SURVIVAL STRATEGIES
A Guide for Turbulent Times

Publishing Since 1978

James E. Neal, Jr.

Neal Publications, Inc.
127 West Indiana Avenue
P.O. Box 451
Perrysburg, OH 43552-0451

Publishers of
Effective Phrases for Performance Appraisals
A Guide for Successful Evaluations
The #1 Guide to Performance Appraisals: Doing It Right!
*Effective Letters for Business, Professional
and Personal Use*
A Guide for Successful Correspondence

Library of Congress Control Number: 2003115369

ISBN 1-882423-63-1
SAH 240-8198

Job Survival Strategies
A Guide for Turbulent Times

Neal Publications, Inc.
127 West Indiana Avenue
P.O. Box 451
Perrysburg, Ohio 43552-0451

First Edition   2004

Cover Image: Getty Images®

This publication is designed to provide accurate and authori-
tative information in regard to the subject matter covered. It
is sold with the understanding that the publisher is not
engaged in rendering legal, accounting, or other professional services. If legal advice or other expert assistance is
required, the services of a competent professional person
should be sought.

CONTENTS

1 The New Corporation 1
2 Recognizing Troubled Companies 7
3 Making Smart Educational Choices 15
4 Knowing Your Job Security Level 19
5 Identifying Personal Danger Signals . . .25
6 Becoming a Vital Employee 33
7 Excelling in Management Skills 53
8 Encouraging Delegation 69
9 Increasing Job Security with
   Knowledge 77
10 Communicating for Greater Job
   Security 85
11 Managing Time 93
12 Keeping Up with Technology 97
13 Displaying Ethics and Loyalty 101
14 Realizing the Importance of Performance
   Appraisals 107
15 Using Entrenpreneurship as a
   Safety Net 113
16 Adding It Up .117

FOREWORD

Never before in American history has corporate life been more turbulent.

Acquisitions, mergers, bankruptcies, downsizing, global outsourcing, greater workloads, and longer hours have all created highly stressful and uncertain job security.

This book is designed to help employees cope through strategies that will provide more job protection. Some of the material is adopted from the author's book titled *Effective Phrases for Performance Appraisals,* which has appeared on a number of best-seller lists. The author has also drawn heavily from many years of management experience both with a large international firm and as a successful entrepreneur.

Quotation marks are used to place emphasis and do not reflect actual statements.

It is hoped that the thoughts in this book will greatly assist you in achieving a prosperous and more secure future.

THE NEW
CORPORATION

For many decades, individuals joined a corporation and remained for thirty years or more. Substantial retirement benefits accrued. A corporate culture existed similar to a large family.

The founder stayed active and would never consider selling the firm. Second generations eventually took control and kept operations stable. Third generations were eager to "cash in" and sell the company.

Today, mature markets and global competition are making it more difficult to raise prices. Ongoing cost-cutting programs have become standard operating procedure. Saturated markets are forcing companies to grow through acquisitions and mergers rather than revenues alone.

America is now in a new era. The positive economic forces that supported the U.S. economy in previous decades are no longer present.

Major retailers are placing tremendous pressures on suppliers for lower prices. Suppliers, in turn, are unable to achieve significant cost reductions while producing in the United States. As a result, plants in the United States are closing as manufacturing moves overseas.

Many believe that the changes in the workplace are the greatest since America converted from an agricultural to an industrial economy.

The average performance of the past is no longer sufficient to attain success in a global economy. Employment security is being dramatically affected by a number of factors.

Shareholders now demand bottom-line performance. As a result, turnover among CEOs is rapidly increasing. New managements perform clean sweeps, and long-term relationships and policies are promptly changed.

New advertising agencies are hired. Pensions, health care benefits, and 401(k) programs are often downgraded. Employee co-payments are increased. Retirement plans are reduced. Departments and positions are eliminated. Unprofitable plants and stores are closed.

Technology is having a tremendous impact on employee security. Companies are replacing workers with computers and machines that do not require health insurance or annual raises. Who would have ever imagined that cash registers could instantly transmit sales to company headquarters? Who would have ever thought that inventories could be tracked up to the minute allowing automatic ordering and just-in-time deliveries? Did you know that automated machines are being tested to replace grocery baggers at supermarkets?

If you lock your keys inside one of today's cars, there may be no need to call a locksmith. One telephone call can unlock your car by satellite.

Outsourcing provides numerous cost-cutting benefits to a company. Fixed costs are changed to variable costs. By outsourcing many administrative functions, companies are able to focus on their core competencies that generate revenues and profits.

The use of part-time and temporary employees previously limited to retailing is now spreading throughout all corporate areas. Temporary persons once confined to receptionists, clerks, and manual laborers are increasingly found in middle and lower management. Positions such as engineers, computer programmers, and tax professionals are being filled with temporaries. Temporary consultants are often retained when face-to-face terminations are required.

The selling world has not escaped changes. Internet sales continue to grow. Consumers are bypassing retailers and ordering directly from manufacturers. Computerized inventory control has eliminated the need for sales persons to physically search shelves for out-of-stock items.

Web sites are providing detailed product information that was once available only from sales persons. Individuals using the web can be more knowledgeable than a sales person in a new car dealership.

Sales to large retail chains are increasingly being handled by executives at a company's headquarters without the participation of local field sales personnel. Retailers are becoming increasingly consolidated, and the job security of many field sales representatives is diminishing.

Customer service is being handled directly by manufacturers using 800 numbers and computer voice options. Who is not familiar with the computer voice that says, "Please select from the following options," options that include everything except what you want to know? Or this message: "We're sorry, all of our representatives are currently assisting other customers"?

Politicians seem helpless in confronting the growing number of jobs that are escaping abroad. Most of these jobs have been in manufacturing and telephone calling operations. Today, however, exported jobs are spreading to a broader range of white-collar workers.

Fiber optic cables have made it possible for companies to fill high-paying domestic positions with employees who are located overseas. You cannot tell whether you are talking to a person across the street or across the world. X-rays taken in the United States are now being read by overseas doctors.

A large corporation can hire several engineers in China or India at a cost equal to one engineer in the United States. India has some of the world's most respected technical schools. Gaining admission is extremely difficult for students, and graduates are in worldwide demand. India has become a recruiting ground for U.S. software manufacturers.

China is capturing the production floors while India is going after the offices in the United States.

Once a firm hires low cost overseas employees to support domestic operations, competitors are forced to do likewise, and the practice spreads throughout the economy.

America's trade gap is probably the most serious factor affecting U.S. employment. Domestic companies are finding it increasingly difficult to compete with goods manufactured in foreign countries. Overseas manufacturers not only provide much lower wages but also are not required to meet strict environmental and other government regulations.

You can never assume that your employer will not transfer manufacturing operations to foreign countries. Some of the nation's oldest companies, including popular brand name manufacturers of television sets and blue jeans, no longer produce in the states.

Unlike decades ago, unions are placing a top priority on job security. Contracts are now addressing the issues of technology and transfer of work to outside suppliers and overseas plants.

As markets become more competitive, companies are placing greater emphasis on the "hard" functions of business—namely manufacturing, finance, and sales. All functions that directly contribute to the bottom line are given priority.

Firms are favoring action rather than analysis. Bureaucracy and layers of middle management are being eliminated to increase earnings.

Nonprofit organizations such as charities and libraries are also under strong pressure to increase productivity with fewer employees.

Today's corporations are like chips in a poker game. They are continuously changing hands and many employees are being lost in the shuffle.

In short, people are losing job security as the corporate world changes and technology accelerates. The total sum of all these developments is creating persistent job anxiety among workers, families, and communities.

RECOGNIZING TROUBLED COMPANIES

During the 50s, 60s and 70s American corporations experienced steady growth. Annual growth objectives of 10 percent were common. Corporations rapidly expanded their organizations both horizontally and vertically. Whenever a person retired, promotions would occur throughout the organization. If the president retired, a person would be hired in the mailroom.

TERMINATING EMPLOYEES

Today, each vacancy provides an opportunity to eliminate a position. The first action of companies in trouble is to cut people.

Downsizing feeds upon itself. Distressed companies waste no time in notifying financial analysts of their downsizing programs. The analysts in turn applaud the companies for their bold action, and higher stock prices soon follow. The financial publicity and stock recommendations encourage more companies to take similar measures.

In cases where an employee is replaced, companies are increasingly recruiting from the outside. They often prefer someone with fresh ideas and new insights. With opportunities for upward mobility declining, organizations will be facing a tremendous challenge. How will they attract and keep competent people as promotional opportunities become increasingly limited? By the same token, how will career-oriented persons achieve job security in a turbulent environment?

Organizations can be brutal in handling capable and veteran employees. Assume you are the head of a marketing or manufacturing department with thirty employees. Your performance is documented as excellent and your group is encountering no problems.

Over a period of one year, responsibilities are gradually transferred out of your department, for sometimes political rather than business reasons. One day your boss calls you in and says that the company can no longer afford to pay your salary because it is not commensurate with your reduced responsibilities. You can't believe that this is the ultimate pay-off for your many years of dedicated and distinguished service.

Another example of organizational insensitivity occurs whenever a long-term employee is suddenly called to the human resources office to be terminated and "read their rights" to a severance program. A security officer is then called to escort the veteran employee to his or her office to clean out their desk and leave the building within one hour. The company graciously provides a number of cardboard boxes, and computer passwords are immediately changed.

Terminated employees with many years of service are increasingly likely to go to court charging wrongful discharge or violations of federal and state discrimination laws.

Outplacement has become one of the fastest growing areas of the human resources field. Companies would prefer to have terminated employees spend their time at outplacement offices rather than at attorney offices filing lawsuits.

In some companies, reorganizations have become a yearly and predictable event. Managements tend to reorganize during the months of October and November. While terminations have ruined the holidays of many former employees, it enables a company to inform shareholders and the financial community that management is well positioned to capitalize on all opportunities during the coming year.

Companies seem to truly believe that each reorganization will provide the long-sought solution to their problems. Employees in ever-changing organizations are under continuous stress. They never know where they stand.

Civic disgust is increasing in industrial America. Corporations who close plants are finding more state and local governments contemplating lawsuits charging breach of contract. After making costly infrastructure improvements for the benefit of local plants, cities are fighting back to prevent factory shutdowns. Granting special loans at highly favorable rates and tax concessions are other reasons for communities to expect a payback. The problem has become so serious that bills have been introduced in the U.S. Congress concerning penalties for companies that move plants overseas.

In view of these increasingly common scenarios and the continuous restructuring of U.S. organizations, it's obvious why morale and loyalty are fast declining among American workers. The situation is happening at a time when the nation needs the best-dedicated efforts of all workers in order to compete in a global economy.

MONITORING YOUR EMPLOYER

Employees have a close and vested interest in the performance of their employers. It is vital that job security-oriented employees keep a sharp eye on their employers. When companies lose their momentum, a number of warning signs begin to appear.

Signs of corporate trouble often appear earlier in smaller companies. In a closely knit group, company performance is well known. Inventories build up. There is less activity in the order department, and fewer trucks are seen leaving the shipping dock. Often, there is a feeling of uneasiness throughout the company.

Visual identification of approaching problems is more difficult in large companies. Inventories are scattered in different plants. Sales and profits may vary considerably among product lines. The company's condition may only be available from investment services and annual reports.

If your company is listed on a stock exchange, you want to thoroughly review the annual reports. If you are not a shareholder, you can request a copy from the firm's investor or public relations department. Keep in mind that annual reports are often embellished.

Here's a clever strategy for learning more about your employer: go to a large public library where you can review recent investment reports, and you may learn of the company's desire to spin off certain divisions, operations, or product lines. Information of this type will seldom appear in the annual report or other company communications.

A decline in earnings is often the first indicator of trouble. Stock dividends are cut. The price of the stock falls. Facilities and divisions are sold in an effort to boost profits. Contributions to charitable organizations are sharply reduced. Pension funds may be tapped as a quick source of cash.

Overcontrol sets in and more intracompany billing becomes common practice. Departments start billing other departments. As an example, the Information Processing group bills Office Services for mainframe support. Office Services, in turn, starts to bill Information Processing for electricity, heat, and depreciation. Before long, a monstrous intracompany billing bureaucracy is established, causing the loss of productivity at an added cost to the company.

Financial people often take control of companies in trouble. Budgets become so complicated that a small purchase must be allocated to a variety of accounts and departments. Advertising and sales promotion are frequently cut to "save money." Sales forces are often reduced.

When too many people are employed, emphasis shifts to reporting. In the marketing area, routine sales call reports become major presentations.

Weekly sales reports are changed to daily reports. Valuable selling time is lost as more attention is given to control and internal administration.

Simple e-mails become dissertations. Quarterly reports become bimonthly reports. More memos are written to the file to cover oneself. Computer space becomes cluttered.

Routine telephone calls become conference calls. Speakerphones begin to appear throughout the office.

Meetings become conferences. Field sales managers are increasingly called to headquarters to attend a conference. More and larger conference rooms are needed.

Committees become task forces. Individual responsibility and authority are transferred to groups. Everyone is protecting themselves. Leadership declines and the entire organization becomes stagnant.

Symbolic measures are taken such as curtailing or eliminating company picnics and holiday gifts. Family-oriented programs such as flexible time schedules and telecommuting may be eliminated. Troubled companies in times of high unemployment no longer need to provide family assistance programs to attract and retain workers.

Staffs are significantly cut. Everyone wonders who will be next. Productivity drops as people lose sleep and complain of health problems.

A hiring freeze at lower levels is announced. Salary increases and bonuses are reduced or eliminated. Out-of-town consultants are called in.

Executives are hired from the outside, bypassing capable employees who guided the company during its period of greatest growth. Tremendous amounts of time are spent in "streamlining" the organization.

Managements become preoccupied with quarterly results and avoid long-range planning. Top executives may become protective and work for their own best interests rather than for shareholders. Morale drops dramatically and the spirit of a once proud company is shattered.

ELIMINATING OVERSTAFFING

Overstaffing is clearly one of the fundamental contributions to the downfall of troubled organizations. A surplus of employees not only siphons off profits but decreases individual productivity. It must be recognized, however, that the same organizations taking pride in their own downsizing efforts are the very same firms who created the staffs in order to "strengthen their organizations."

In an overstaffed environment, people are continuously trying to justify their existence. Persons can become experts at "make work" projects. Some individuals have mastered the art of making junk mail reading look important.

One of the sure signs of an overstaffed company is the widespread use of assistants. As soon as one executive obtains an assistant, you can be sure that other executives will seek similar positions. Unless assistants can be assigned to specific areas of responsibility, they often become excess baggage to a company. A sales manager, for example, will take a new assistant on calls to meet the accounts. However, joint calls soon become standard practice at a considerable added expense to the company.

Effective managers do not overstaff and strive to keep jobs meaningful and challenging. They realize that a disgruntled or bored employee can display attitudes that negatively influence co-workers and customers. Top managers use lateral moves to spark new interests and motivate the entire organization.

In any organization, many persons, especially those with higher educations, will admit that they are not working at their fullest potential. They are capable of handling more responsibility and making a greater contribution.

We frequently read of companies that release hundreds or thousands of workers. Yet the enterprises continue to function. You cannot help but wonder about the contributions of the persons who were terminated and never replaced.

Smart companies no longer adhere to human resource policies that encourage the hiring of unnecessary people. Salary classifications were once commonly based on the number of people supervised. Today, managers are often rewarded for reducing staff.

Progressive firms are beginning to realize that the manager who can operate effectively with a smaller staff is a better executive than the person who views more people as the solution to all problems. Managers need to be given additional incentives including monetary rewards for keeping staffs trim.

The ability to produce profitable results with a lean organization will be a major measurement of performance and job security in the years ahead.

MAKING SMART
EDUCATIONAL
CHOICES

Every day in America highly educated college graduates rise and go to work. Instead of settling into an office chair, they are saying, "Do you want fries with that?" Other graduates are working as clerks selling shirts next to co-workers who have only high school educations.

College graduates are pouring out of the nation's universities and colleges majoring in subjects that are not marketable in today's economy. Majoring in philosophy may provide tremendous inner satisfaction, but being able to effectively apply that knowledge in the foreseeable economic environment is questionable.

At the other end of the career path are older engineers, for example, who have lost their jobs due to restructuring programs. These formerly high-paid employees may be found clerking in a local home improvement store.

The popularity of "communications" as a college major is bewildering. The author and his wife frequently dine in college town restaurants across the nation. Whenever we ask about the college major of the server, it seems that more than half will say "communications." We find it hard to believe that communications majors can realistically expect to get a job in communications. One cannot help but wonder if the academic community is promoting communications in order to preserve teaching positions and courses.

Choosing the right career path has never been more critical. A strong case can be made for selecting dual majors that may have lifelong benefits.

Community colleges and vocational schools were once looked upon as institutions for students who could not meet the requirements of accredited universities and colleges. Students graduating from vocational schools with specialized and practical training are now in great demand.

Smart young people will look upon themselves as entrepreneurs. They will merely apply their entrepreneurial skills while working for an employer. Since many jobs and career changes are likely, they need to acquire effective and practical skills that are applicable to various employment challenges.

MAKING CAREER CHOICES

In choosing a career, young persons need to recognize some broad and major factors that will affect future job security. One of the most critical factors influencing the employment market is the aging population. Baby boomers will soon be retiring, creating tremendous markets—especially in healthcare. The healthcare market promises strong job security for many years to come.

Certified automotive technicians can get a job any-where in the nation. Persons graduating in nursing and specialized medical technology are in strong demand. Some of the most secure jobs in the nation are presently the following:

Nurses

Pharmacists

Medical Technicians

Physical Therapists

High School Teachers in math and science

Morticians

Technology is severely affecting many occupations that previously enjoyed solid job security. Graphic art and commercial art studios, for example, were once major suppliers to the nation's corporations. These outside suppliers employed rows of artists that would prepare in a variety of colors the materials needed for speeches, presentations and reports. Today, a well-trained secretary with powerful software can produce graphics that once required many hours of manual preparation.

For many years, big corporations employed large travel departments. In-house personnel arranged all travel. Today's executives now use the Internet to schedule all transportation and lodging reservations. They have a boarding pass in hand before leaving the building.

Persons who tour overseas manufacturing plants are shocked by the absence of workers. Robots dominate acres of production floors.

Manufacturing jobs have steadily declined in the United States while output has risen. We are simply becoming more productive. Computers are now running everything from landing airplanes to piloting cruise ships.

The number of farmers in the United States has dropped dramatically since the early 1900s, but America now grows enough crops to supply our domestic demand and much of the world's.

The foregoing examples clearly point out the urgent need to keep abreast of trends affecting job security. Employed persons simply have to look five years ahead for factors that may be detrimental to their job security. Technological changes can wipe out jobs regardless of how well they are being performed.

As we become a service-oriented economy, many occupations are being upgraded. In many states, pharmacists are now consulting, and physician assistants are being given more authority.

The social economic structure involving occupations is reflected in large-city country club memberships. If you look at membership rosters from thirty years ago, you will find that the greatest majority of members were corporate executives and professional persons. Today, entrepreneurs in areas such as accounting, auditing, car sales, construction, electrical contracting, computer specialists, plumbing, real estate, refrigeration, and professional persons dominate memberships.

A secure job is a major worry for most Americans. Smart employees will keep fully aware of ongoing market forces that are occurring in the present and future economic environment.

KNOWING YOUR JOB SECURITY LEVEL

To achieve greater job protection, it's important to recognize that most careers comprise three levels of security:

The Dream.........1st decade
The Realties.......2nd decade
The Hanging In .3rd decade

When you are beginning your career, the whole world is your oyster. You feel that you will work hard and you will surely get your rewards. You are bubbling with enthusiasm. You seize every opportunity and are eager to taste success.

Job security at this stage is mixed. On the one hand, your employer may believe that you are an ideal candidate for replacing a much higher-paid employee at a considerably lower salary. On the other hand, the employer may be of the opinion that they have little invested in you, and you may be easily terminated at no loss to the company.

During the second decade, you begin to realize the realties of organizational life—not everyone can be job proof.

If you are fortunate, a promotion may come your way. Promotions are one of life's most rewarding experiences and provide a real sense of well-being.

Your bargaining power may never be greater than at the time of a true promotion. A newly appointed person may be able to obtain requests that would be totally unrealistic after spending some time in the new job.

One normally accepts all promotions. However, sometimes there are situations that make promotions undesirable. Aside from personal reasons, you may wish to think twice before accepting a high-risk position. A typical high-risk situation would be a nebulous position such as a "special assignment" in which previous occupants have been consistently terminated.

Your bargaining power during the third decade is normally nonexistent. Your benefit programs have locked you in, and many employers would welcome your resignation. You are now in the high-risk area. Companies are eager to eliminate your position or replace you with a person earning a substantially lower salary.

IDENTIFYING SENIOR EMPLOYEE CONCERNS

Throughout the third decade, a senior employee must be wary of major changes in the company's employee evaluation system. A long-term employee may have many years of excellent reviews. In an effort to maintain morale and salary increases, performance appraisals may become highly inflated.

In recognition of deceptively inflated ratings, companies often respond by changing the entire review system. In effect, they want to start over again. Some firms have gone to the controversial system of forced ratings where employee performance is categorized into groups. An example of this is a system where only 20 percent of employees are rated "excellent."

Older employees need to be especially alert to any drastic changes in their performance reviews. Major changes often occur when a person is assigned a new supervisor. If necessary, performance objections should be immediately challenged, preferably in writing.

With more and more corporations cutting staff, employees with many years of service are often being cast aside to meet personnel reduction goals. Statements of "elected to retire" often mean "elected not to be fired."

A common tactic is for employers to take all meaningful responsibility away from senior employees. After decades of making important contributions to the organization, the absence of responsibility can be psychologically devastating. Affected employees often become extremely bitter and openly convey their feeling to other employees and the general public. It is amazing how long-term employees can become very bitter toward their employers.

A tragedy of organizational life is that managements often keep a person stymied in the same position for lengthy periods and then wonder why that senior employee is not displaying a positive and enthusiastic attitude toward the job after a decade of performing the same duties.

Older employees tend to follow one or two distinct patterns. Employee A, for example, will display the following characteristics:

1. He or she fights the aging process.
2. He may start drinking too much.
3. His thinking is dominated by past experiences rather than future challenges.
4. He avoids all learning experiences.
5. He no longer delegates but becomes totally involved in details to justify his existence and reinforce his self-image.
6. He may become bitter about the organization and its future.

On the other hand, Employee B displays the following traits:

1. He or she graciously accepts their advancing age.
2. He combines his depth of experience with a keen insight for solving present problems and planning for the future.
3. He views his role as an elder statesman and concentrates on developing people rather than performing tasks.
4. He enjoys being a mentor.
5. He delegates extensively.
6. He devotes increasing time to planning for retirement.

What is happening across America is that some salaried employees who wish to retire early are "hanging in," hoping that their employer will eliminate their jobs and offer a liberal retirement-inducement program along with severance pay. A thirty-year employee may be given two week's pay for every year of service, equaling an extra year's worth of salary, which can be a nice bonus for foreign travel or other enjoyment or investment. Terminated employees may also be eligible for unemployment compensation

Employees who are waiting for special retirement incentives are restricting opportunities for younger workers. The situation is becoming a growing problem for the many thousands of college students who graduate every year.

IDENTIFYING PERSONAL DANGER SIGNALS

Despite your best efforts, circumstances beyond your control may lead to job problems with your employer. Early indications of pending job trouble include the following:

1. You are no longer invited to meetings.
2. You are receiving fewer and fewer e-mails and copies of correspondence.
3. Your opinions and ideas are no longer being sought.
4. You are communicating less with your superior.
5. You are increasingly bored.
6. You are passed over for promotions, salary increases, seminar attendance, etc.
7. Your responsibilities are being decreased.
8. Your staff is being reduced.
9. Your office or work station is being moved to a less-desirable location.

10. You are no longer receiving challenging assignments.

11. You are accumulating one year's experience many times.

12. You dread your performance review.

13. You go home not feeling good about yourself.

When any of the above first start to appear, you want to nip them in the bud. The key point to emphasize is that you are capable of making a greater contribution to the success of the enterprise.

It is a lot easier to get an undesirable situation corrected early in its development than wait until problems become deeply entrenched. A combination of problems will eventually present a negative situation that can be insurmountable.

BUILDING A SECURE IMAGE

Successful people project an image of competence. They earn sound reputations and practice effective work habits.

However, organizational life is filled with potential pitfalls. Persons often drift into undesirable work styles without fully recognizing their behavior. They can become easy targets for dismissal.

Every organization has people whose job security is being damaged by negative and stereotyped images. Strategic planning for job security requires that you avoid a reputation for the following.

The Egomaniac

Egomaniacs often confuse activity with accomplishment. They believe that the world revolves around them, and they must always be the center of attention. Egomaniacs usually speak in a loud voice and can frequently be heard ordering secretaries to arrange for tee-off times, hair appointments, and other personal matters. Egomaniacs are the type of people who like to belittle porters, bellhops, and waiters. They may also show little concern for cost control and enjoy making a big production out of little things.

Egomaniacs thrive on cell phones. They can be on the phone before leaving their driveways. Every phone call conveys self-importance, even if they are just ordering a pizza.

Persons with big egos often show more concern about increasing their status than contributing to the betterment of the business or organization. People with huge egos are overly concerned about titles, office size, furniture, carpeting, cars, parking spaces, clubs, and other status symbols.

The author was once aware of a situation where an executive was seen after hours comparing the square feet of a counterpart's office with his office using a tape measure!

Smart managers maintain control over their egos and those of subordinates. They make certain that all perks are evenly distributed among persons with the same level of responsibility. Secure managers take pride in accomplishments rather than status symbols.

The Complainer

Complainers are never content. They start the day complaining about the weather and their health and then go to work where they complain about everything else. Complainers always believe that the grass is greener elsewhere.

Sometimes a manager just wants to say, "Look, if you don't like this or that, why don't you look for another job?"

The author once saw a sign in an office that left a lasting impression. It said, "Remember, the loudest boos always come from those in the free seats!" Security-minded individuals avoid complaining.

The Joker

The joker is the office comedian. You can always count on this person to have the latest joke. By closely watching the late-night shows, the joker makes the office rounds spreading the latest humor. Others feel compelled to spend the time passing the humor on to co-workers. The constant joker belongs in a comedy club, not in a professional setting.

The Bookie

This person is obsessed with gambling. You can count on the bookie to know the very latest odds on a variety of sporting events. They take great pride in owning wireless electronic devices that provide the very latest sporting news and odds. Weekly lotteries are favorites of the bookie. The office bookie is ripe for a career change in a more appropriate field.

The Drifter

The drifter does not understand basic organization. He or she will wonder into all areas outside their responsibilities. Give drifters a little authority, and they will shatter all resemblance to organizational structure.

Managers must keep drifters under constant supervision. Well-written job descriptions with strict enforcement provide the best means of controlling drifters.

The Do-It-Yourselfer

This person handles everything regardless of their job level. No job is too small for the do-it-yourselfer. These people are totally involved with details and often work long hours. They simply cannot delegate and fail to make proper use of staff personnel.

Companies do not promote the do-it-yourselfer. They keep this type of person in specialized staff positions where they will not have the opportunity to underutilize staff personnel.

The Overdelegator

Some people delegate too much. In fact, they often become more of a mail distribution clerk than a manager. Overdelegation can indicate that a person is over qualified for the job or merely has a tendency to transfer responsibility.

The best managers retain some functions that are not delegated. These personal tasks usually involve organizational planning, salary administration, performance evaluation, and budget control.

The Hot Shot

Hot shots produce for effect rather than substance. They will get an idea and create a tremendous amount of furor. They will schedule numerous meetings and generate piles of correspondence. Clerical workers will be taken away from their essential jobs in order to devote full attention to the new project. The entire organization becomes aware of the fury surrounding the project.

After hundreds of hours of work and full-blown presentations, the project or program fails to gain support and just fades away. The once-great idea becomes a bookshelf relic.

The "Yes" Person

Everyone knows the traditional "yes" person. The boss can always count on this individual to provide instant positive reinforcement. The "yes" person always agrees and concurs. "Yes, sir," . . . "Yes, ma'am," . . . "You bet" . . . that's their trademark.

"Yes" people have no place in a sophisticated business environment. Bosses want genuine opinions based on facts. They want to know alternative options and solutions. If you are a manager, encourage honest and objective opinions and avoid being insulated from reality.

The "Status Quo" Person

Individuals who fit this category resist change. They are totally oblivious to new technology, automation, computerization, product life cycles, changing consumer demand, etc. Resistance to change will virtually guarantee less job security.

Managers realize that companies cannot stand still and must move with the times to remain competitive. Effective managers retain persons with open-minded attitudes and encourage the flow of fresh ideas, thoughts, and concepts.

The Librarian

The librarian is continuously reading, subscribing to all kinds of publications that do not necessary relate to the job's specific responsibilities. Out-of-town newspapers are favorite reading material for self-appointed librarians.

Companies use newspaper-clipping services as the best source for obtaining information relevant to the firm or field. While everyone must be kept informed, it's best to restrict subscriptions to publications that clearly relate to an individual's specific function. Reading during business hours should be highly selective and relevant to job responsibilities.

The Joiner

The joiner belongs to a wide variety of professional, charitable, political, and community organizations. Life to the joiner is a series of meetings, breakfasts, brunches, lunches, and dinners. The joiner considers a home in the same light as a hotel. The joiner is often searching for recognition and challenges that are not present in the normal work situation.

Progressive firms expect their employees to be civic minded and take an active role in community affairs. However, outside activities need to be kept in perspective and not substituted for a job as the outlet for one's primary energies.

The Traveler

This person relates success to travel. He or she does not believe in telephones or e-mails. They will travel to the other side of the country on a moment's notice. The airlines love "the traveler." Although face-to-face discussions have their value, effective executives make good use of the telephone and conference calls while limiting travel to actual need.

The Convention, Show, or Conference Goer

This person is the first to sign up for a convention, show, or other function in the industry or field. Attractive locations and climates are always preferred. By attending so many functions, this person will eventually be assigned to various committees, task forces, etc. Industry recognition tends to thrive upon itself, resulting in an increasing number of committee assignments in allied organizations.

Top managers recognize that active involvement in industry or professional organizations is essential to maintaining competency. However, excessive involvement often indicates deeper problems. The person's priorities may have become misguided, and he or she may be devoting insufficient time to the job. The person may simply be bored and need new challenges and opportunities.

In summary, a success-oriented person strives to develop a well-balanced image conveying competence and stature.

Negative images are deadly in organizational life. They make you a prime target for termination. Make every effort to be known as a positive person with sound work habits.

BECOMING A
VITAL EMPLOYEE

ACCEPTING YOUR PERSONALITY

Your personality reflects the sum total of life's experiences since birth. Basic personality traits normally remain constant.

Aside from restructuring programs, it is generally accepted that more persons are terminated from their jobs because of underlying personality conflicts and communication problems than technical incompetence. Persons with abrasive personalities can be especially disruptive to the smooth operation of an organization.

While you cannot generally change your basic personality, you can make every effort to display a cheerful and pleasing disposition. You can also strive to convey calm, even temperament and friendly attitude.

Organizations place a high premium on positive persons. No matter how difficult the situation or circumstance, the accepted response must always be positive. Many careers have been ruined because a person was labeled as a negative thinker.

Before you can convey positive impressions to others, you must have a high self-esteem. You have certain strengths and successes that can be drawn upon to generate good, positive feelings about yourself.

From the moment that you arrive at work, you want to radiate positive attitudes filled with optimism. When everyone is complaining about the weather, you want to be the person who states that the rain will help the flowers, or the snow will be great for the skiers. You want to turn every lemon into lemonade.

WORKING HARMONIOUSLY AND EFFECTIVELY WITH OTHERS

Your ability to get along with people is vital to your job security. You can be the most capable person in your organization, but you need to interact harmoniously with people to be effective. When retrenchment programs arise, managers want to retain individuals who have the ability to work well with others and inspire a team effort.

Team-building skills are critical in modern management. Being a star team player is essential to your job security. A person who earns a reputation as a good team member will be assigned to a growing number of important projects.

Try not to be overassertive. Although the subject of assertiveness has sold many self-help books, there is a real danger that the person who emphasizes assertive behavior will be labeled as an aggressive troublemaker.

Discussions between business people are often an exercise in assertiveness. With so many people making comments such as "If I understand correctly . . . ," it's easy to become more interested in the verbal crossfire than the purpose of the discussion.

You want to develop a reputation for being able to get along with your superiors, peers, and subordinates. Be firm, friendly, and cordial to everyone, and demonstrate that you are a very positive member of the team.

Above all, always be straightforward and honest.

WINNING WITH MOTIVATION

Motivated persons are committed to achieving results. They strive for excellence and maximum effectiveness. They build on individual strengths and display a strong achievement drive.

Motivated people are success oriented, and they capitalize on all opportunities. They are ambitious, hardworking, and quickly rebound from disappointment. They generate positive attitudes and spark enthusiasm.

People are motivated by both inner and external goals. Some persons pursue goals for the sake of professional accomplishment and personal satisfaction. Others seek goals for materialistic and monetary awards. The key to keeping motivated is to pursue a goal that gets you fired up regardless of the nature.

True achievers take tremendous pride in their accomplishments. They derive great satisfaction from achieving excellence in making a presentation, writing a report, or obtaining a large order. The feeling of doing something with perfection is one of life's greatest satisfactions.

Success-oriented people develop the habit of winning. When one goal is reached, they strive for another. They are self-starters and obtain enormous satisfaction through hard work, commitment, and accomplishment. The ability to attain results for personal satisfaction will ultimately benefit the organization and return many rewards.

Because your thoughts govern your actions, try to associate with enthusiastic people. Positive people radiate energy and provide inspiration to everyone who comes in contact with them. Enthusiasm is contagious.

The one trait that really distinguishes the best superiors is the desire to accomplish results without being concerned about who gets credit. Big bosses build people and they do think big!

Organizations place a very high value on motivation. Have you ever noticed that motivational speakers almost always appear on the program at conventions, banquets, etc?

Executives who are truly people oriented use recognition to motivate. They make effective use of awards, certificates, ribbons, etc. Recognizing individuals for outstanding performance before others and large groups is a time-proven method for motivating people.

Motivation moves the world and your career. Strive to project a very positive and enthusiastic image.

Just as you load up a computer, you can load up your brain with enthusiastic and positive thoughts.

Remember the words of Emerson: "Nothing great was ever achieved without enthusiasm."

TAKING THE INITIATIVE

People with initiative are self-starters. They carry out assignments with little or no direction. They are solution seekers and demonstrate an ability to think constructively. They are resourceful and self-reliant, and they take charge.

Initiative is one of your best tickets to job security. The opportunities for displaying initiative are always present.

You want to demonstrate to your superiors that you are forward looking and would welcome an opportunity to contribute to the development of the annual marketing plan, profitability plan, etc.

By taking the initiative, you relieve your superior of many details. Temporary assignments offer excellent opportunities to demonstrate your ability and value to the company.

It is better to take the initiative and be told that you are out of line than to always maintain the status quo. You are sending a message whenever you display initiative.

Initiative is the spirit of enterprise.

ESTABLISHING DEPENDABILITY

Dependability is a key trait that is highly respected and appreciated by every manager. A reputation for dependability must be earned over a period of time.

Dependable persons are punctual. They are consistently on time throughout the entire day.

A valued trait is to honor all promises. Try not to make commitments that you cannot fulfill.

Superiors too often take dependability for granted. It's a good practice to occasionally remind your superiors of the special efforts, overtime, etc., that were required to complete a project or meet a deadline.

You want to tactfully convey the image that the loss of your skills would be a serious problem for the company.

CONVEYING PROFESSIONALISM

To be a professional person, you have to act like one. Your appearance and demeanor say a lot about you.

All organizations have written or unwritten dress standards, and you certainly want to conform. Casual business wear is currently losing its popularity in favor of more formal dress. Choose your wardrobe carefully and place heavy emphasis on conservative colors such as dark blue, gray, and white. Despite fads, traditional clothing always seems to return.

It's better to have a smaller wardrobe of quality clothing than a large wardrobe of lesser quality. When you arrive at home after work, change your clothes to reduce wear. Always keep your clothes well pressed.

If in doubt about how to dress for a specific occasion, always overdress. You will feel very uncomfortable being the only person at a function without a suit on. Formal clothing conveys class.

Wear jewelry and accessories in moderation. Good grooming is essential, and wear a hairstyle reasonably consistent with organizational practice.

A good physical appearance is a major plus in today's business world. The time and effort spent in developing a good physical appearance may not only make you healthier but may very well increase your earnings potential.

Another good investment is to keep a smile on your face—it costs nothing, but can pay big dividends.

Appearance also applies to your work area. Make every effort to keep your desk or office neat and businesslike. The display of personal items such as photographs should be kept to a minimum. Decorations and accessories should reflect your professional interests and accomplishments.

Successful people convey confidence and high energy by maintaining good posture. They walk at a brisk pace with their head up and back straight. Success-oriented persons always appear to be on an important mission whether it's going to a board meeting or to the drinking fountain.

In short, you want to cultivate executive stature and project a positive image of professional competence.

GROWING THROUGH VERSATILITY

Persons who enjoy strong job security tend to have the ability to perform a wide range of assignments and display skills in adapting to changing conditions. People with versatile skills are highly valued by every department head.

You can develop versatility by making every effort to perform as many varied assignments as possible. Special assignments and projects offer excellent opportunities to demonstrate your abilities and broaden your knowledge of the organization.

Versatility can lead to undiscovered talents. Shortly after graduating from college, the author joined a large international corporation and was asked to write a speech for a middle-class executive. The assignment was totally unrelated to my entry-level position. Apparently, I did a good job because other executives were soon asking me to write their speeches.

Before long, I was writing speeches for the highest executives who delivered them at many of the world's largest convention centers. My initial acceptance to write a speech led to an entire career that would never have occurred if I had not assumed an unrelated assignment.

As organizations become leaner, diversified assignments will grow. Companies are becoming more team oriented with emphasis shifting to persons with broad-based backgrounds and experience. Competent persons with the ability to adapt will be the winners of tomorrow.

You have everything to gain by making it known that you are always interested in any horizontal transfer or new responsibilities that will increase your overall knowledge.

You want to avoid tying your job security to any one superior. With management turnover fast increasing, your superior may be terminated at any time, leaving you dead in the water. Make a special effort to respect and maintain good relationships with all persons that are in higher positions at the firm.

Your job security is dependent on your ability to obtain a position with another employer or enter entrepreneurship. Fortunately, the loss of a job due to restructuring no longer carries a negative stigma in today's business world.

Versatility is a key trait because it will open many doors for you. It is vital that you keep your resume up-to-date. People often forget about their successes in handling various responsibilities, which makes a written record essential.

Individuals also tend to underestimate the value of their experience. At some point in time, experiences can be categorized into different areas and thereby provide opportunities for a variety of careers. For example, some resumes can be structured to provide solid backgrounds in advertising, merchandising, or public relations.

Smaller companies generally provide opportunities for acquiring broad and diversified experience. You are less likely to become slotted in a smaller firm.

A versatile background with demonstrated competence in several areas will make you more secure by greatly improving your employability.

GIVING QUALITY TOP PRIORITY

Quality is a prerequisite for greater job security. You can debate the need for quantity, but not quality.

Quality is often associated with a product, but quality of service is equally important. Many product lines are noted for their parity. In some cases, competitive products contain the same raw materials and are manufactured on the same machines by employees in the same union. The greatest difference among products is often packaging, perception, and service.

Customer service often provides a big opportunity for achieving success. Unsurpassed service aimed at customer satisfaction is a winner in every field. By excelling in service, you can't lose in developing satisfied clients, patients, or customers.

Quality is often involved in decision making. It is generally best to decide on a course of action that favors quality. For example, let's assume that a secretary is requested to reserve a hospitality suite in the middle price range at a specific hotel. The hotel advises that hospitality suites are only available in the lower or higher price range. If the secretary is unable to confer with the superior, the best decision is to select the option providing the better quality.

Strive to be known as a quality person. Your work should always reflect your very best. Make every effort to demonstrate professional pride and a strong desire for accuracy, thoroughness, and perfection. When it comes to quality, you want to display a total commitment to excellence.

Quality is achieved by persons who recognize the value of their work in contributing to bigger and broader accomplishments. Individuals who take pride in the ultimate product or service are quality conscious. If you set high quality standards, others will bring their performance up to your expectations.

KEEPING QUANTITY IN PERSPECTIVE

In general, the quantity of your work is not as important as the quality. One idea may be worth more to your employer and your job security than years of tedious work. Selling is a notable exception where quantity of sales is obviously essential for success.

A relatively small portion of each job normally yields the greatest returns. Consequently, you want to target the areas having the greatest impact and devote a high degree of effort to them.

Everyone has a certain time of the day when they are more productive. Plan to devote your prime time to the areas of your job that deliver the biggest payoff.

MAINTAINING CURRENT JOB DESCRIPTIONS

Position descriptions are critical to your job security. Every employee should have a copy of their position description listing responsibilities, duties, and performance criteria.

Most employees are working longer and harder than ever before. Many executives are now working with smaller staffs. Subordinates are often assuming responsibilities that far exceed those outlined in the company's original position description. The fact that your superior is aware of your added responsibilities is not sufficient. In the advent of a retrenchment program, outside consultants may recommend the termination of your boss. As a result, you want to always make sure that your position description filed in the human resources department is continuously updated to reflect your additional responsibilities.

DISPLAYING MATURITY

A mature person displays strong emotional stability and keeps situations in proper perspective. A mature individual makes a strong effort to keep small problems from interfering with job performance.

Some managers display unstable and sometimes irrational behavior that creates an environment of fear. Managers with unpredictable behavior patterns often treat every day and every problem as if it were an emergency. As a result, subordinates and co-workers adopt defensive positions, which destroys initiative.

Life in any organization is a mixture of good and bad days. Organizational life is not all glory, but neither is it all gloom and doom. You must learn to accept reality and display strong emotional control, especially when things are not going well. You want to avoid being the type of person who is always blaming others for their mistakes, misfortunes, or inadequacies.

In any position, you are certain to encounter disappointments. Despite your best efforts, things will not always go your way. How you respond to disappointments is a reflection of your maturity. In such situations, you can either mope about it, or pick up the pieces and move on. The secure person does not enjoy failure but rebounds with greater determination and enthusiasm. Persons who have experienced failure find success particularly sweet.

The author once read about a person whose business went bankrupt. Instead of being totally devastated, he started giving seminars on the subject of bankruptcy. This is truly turning a negative situation into a positive.

HANDLING CRITICISM

Maturity is especially needed when you are being criticized. One test of your strength is how well you act under criticism. In situations involving criticism, you want to firmly state your position, admit all mistakes or errors in judgment, and above all, be honest and maintain emotional control.

Some superiors actually enjoy giving criticism. They derive satisfaction by exerting their power and watching others squirm.

The author once knew of an executive who would always order a steak at a fancy restaurant. He would give specific instructions of how he wanted it cooked. No matter how it was prepared, the executive would always send it back. The server would always get upset, and others at the table would stare in amazement. Secure executives are not complainers.

One of the best methods for handling criticism is to agree with the criticizer. For example, Smith calls Jones into the office and says, "Jones, I am sure that you are aware that the company has a strict policy against first-class air travel. On your recent flight from

New York, you traveled first-class and I must seriously reprimand you. I want to know why you think you can defy company policy and fly first-class!"

The best reply from Jones would be along these lines: "Smith, you are absolutely right. Company policy permits only coach-class air travel. In this particular incident, all the coach-class seats were filled on the last flight of the day so I purchased a first-class ticket. I wanted to get home in time for my daughter's first piano recital. I will be glad to write you a check for the difference."

Agreeing with criticism renders the criticizer ineffective and destroys the opportunity for others to gain ego reinforcement at your expense.

Another sign of a mature person is the ability to maintain confidentiality. In organizational life, there is a great temptation to share confidential information. If your superior entrusts you with confidential material, you have a moral responsibility to remain silent. A reputation for integrity and trustworthiness is one of the finest tributes that you can earn.

Emotion is part of life and certainly affects managerial behavior. The best executives display a balance between being a crisis manager and a happy-go-lucky manager. The key to emotional maturity is to calmly channel your emotions into positive, enthusiastic, and philosophic attitudes.

KEEPING PERSONAL PROBLEMS TO YOURSELF

Smart employees will learn to keep personal problems from affecting their performance and the work of others. Everyone has personal problems, and it is always therapeutic to discuss them with a close friend or two. However, it is totally inappropriate and in poor taste to have an entire office concerned about your toothache or car troubles. Learn to confine your personal problems to yourself or you will develop a reputation for being a weak person who is unable to cope with tough problems.

KEEPING ALCOHOL IN ITS PLACE

Many companies are very sensitive about alcohol consumption. The author has known of a large corporation that would not allow their executives to have a picture taken while holding a glass even if it was just water. In newspapers and the firm's house organ, photographs taken at various functions were often cut so that only the upper bodies were shown!

The business world provides ample opportunities for drinking. Boredom, stress, celebrations, entertainment, travel, country clubs, and expense account living all contribute to a life style that can lead to drinking problems.

Traveling salespersons often check into a hotel and immediately head to the bar. Loneliness seeks company, and drinking among travelers often becomes a problem.

Persons who drink to excess in the presence of other employees can quickly gain a reputation that may have devastating effects on job security. A reputation for drinking can offset years of hard work and many of the fine professional tributes that lead to solid employment.

Organizational life has many pitfalls that are entirely beyond your control but alcohol is not one of them.

MAKING STRESS WORK FOR YOU

Intensified competition in American business is creating more stress in corporate life. Business problems eventually become people problems. In an environment where emphasis is frequently shifting from growth to retrenchment, people become more irritable, critical, and hyper. The trend to greater turnover among top management is contributing to more unsettled behavior in the corporate world.

More and more young people with strong educational backgrounds and high ambitions are competing for fewer middle-class management positions. Meanwhile, legislation has given older workers greater job protection while medical science is increasing life expectancy.

The nation's media is creating more stress by reporting more business news. Cable television is reporting around-the-clock news about possible corporate takeovers, layoffs, and plant closures.

Technology and computers are contributing to a more stressful environment for many employees. Managers can use computers to record the number and time duration of breaks, incoming calls, and computer time. The strict regimentation of employees, combined with greater use of office automation, is certain to dehumanize the work environment and increase the amount of routine operations. Altogether, these factors are creating greater potential for overmanagement and employee stress.

Effective employees manage stress even when confronted with the most difficult circumstances. They successfully cope with multiple demands from superiors, subordinates, and peers. They perform well in crisis situations and handle the unexpected with coolness.

Everyone has different stress levels. Extreme stress to one individual may be nothing more than a minor nuisance to another.

People who are operating under stress frequently display abnormal behavior. They usually amplify excessive traits. A talkative person will become even more talkative under stress, while a quiet person will become even quieter.

Employees who are unable to cope with stress often lose their perspective and become obsessed with details. They divert attention away from important problems and frequently concentrate on trivial matters. For example, an executive under stress may become enraged over a simple typing error.

Managers who cannot cope with stress are often quick to criticize and exert negative influences on the productivity of subordinates. People working for such a manager become gun shy. They will not display initiative and assume greater responsibility for fear of being criticized over trivial matters. As a result, employees become stagnant, and productivity decreases throughout the entire department or organization.

Successful persons have learned to make positive use of stress. They often use humor to relieve stress. A witty remark during a period of high stress can reduce tension and place situations in proper perspective.

The use of stress to achieve positive results is depicted by a story involving two fishing boat captains. One fishing boat always returned to the dock with live fish, while the other boat consistently returned with mostly dead fish. Since live fish commanded a higher price in the marketplace, the captain with the dead fish became quite bewildered. One day, he set out to find the answer . . . and what did he find? The captain with the live fish always threw a couple of threatening cat-fish in the tank to keep the other fish moving and alive! Some stress can stimulate positive action.

You can build your resistance to stress by balancing the demands of your job with your private life and keeping healthy. Managements are becoming increasingly health conscious. Today's CEO is gener-ally not the obese cigar-chewing type typically por-trayed in cartoons. In many offices, the first order of business among top executives on Monday morn-ings is to discuss the weekend athletic or workout activities.

Learn to practice moderation in every phase of your life. Take each day one at a time and treat it as if it were in a separate compartment.

You are as big as the things that bother you. You can grow bigger than your problems.

Hard times pass and big people last!

SOCIALIZING FOR GREATER SUCCESS

Socializing can be very effective in furthering your career development and job security. Whether you are a golfer, tennis player, bridge player, boater, or whatever, the social contacts that you develop with other members of the company can be invaluable in boosting your job protection.

The friendships cultivated on the golf course or ten-nis court carry over into the business world. The early morning greeting for many top executives following a weekend is something like "How did you hit them Saturday?" The author has seen CEOs discuss their weekend golf game hole by hole.

Friendships break down formal barriers and provide increased knowledge and accessibility. Social relationships can give you the inside track.

It's important that you try to socialize with respected members of the company. Your association with positive and highly regarded individuals builds a similar image for you.

On the other hand, you want to avoid socializing with negative people who are always complaining or bad-mouthing the company. Every organization has its share of negative people, and you want to avoid them at all costs.

When it comes to socializing, managers should always treat subordinates equally. Inviting selected subordinates to social events is certain to create hard feelings and should be carefully avoided.

In social situations, be very careful not to make a careless remark that can be taken out of context and cause irreversible job damage.

A well-balanced professional and social life involving other members of the organization is a winning strategy for greater job security.

EXCELLING IN MANAGEMENT SKILLS

As organizational life becomes more turbulent, job security will increasingly depend on your ability to achieve management excellence. You can normally excel in the areas that you enjoy the most.

Every person has strengths and weaknesses that are either inherited or acquired. Although you cannot do anything about your height or the color of your eyes, you can cultivate a number of key management strengths.

The traits covered in this chapter will increase your job security and can be nourished to perfection.

STRATEGIES FOR NEW MANAGERS

Whenever you are promoted to a managerial position, you will want to get a new title, higher salary, and improved benefits. Additionally, you should make certain that you receive all the perks that are customary for the position.

The weeks following a promotion are critical to your continued success. Most people in the organization will assume that you have substantially more authority, and you should do nothing to discourage the notion.

If you are promoted to a newly created position, you have a special opportunity to build the job. If you assume that you have certain responsibilities, it is amazing how many people in the organization will not question your authority. If you can maintain self-assumed authority over a period of time, you will eventually receive formal authority simply because you are the person who handles the responsibility.

While promoted individuals obviously cannot always maintain the same professional relationships, a continuing cordial respect for others will build a supportive team for you.

Persons who are promoted often undergo distinct changes in their relationships with others. An individual may have spent years enjoying coffee breaks with co-workers. He or she may have participated in office betting pools and treated secretaries and other workers with cordial respect.

Once promoted, coffee breaks are viewed as an unnecessary waste of time. The annual World Series pool becomes gambling on company premises. Secretaries are viewed as machine operators and "gofers." Is it any wonder that some promoted persons do not gain the respect and support of others?

When you are promoted, try to maintain the style that got you promoted in the first place. It will demonstrate real class and build your future and job security.

ACQUIRING LEADERSHIP TRAITS

True leaders are committed to principles which guide both individuals and organizations. Leaders display self-confidence, courage, authority, and loyalty. They command the respect of others and inspire cooperation and enthusiasm.

A leader is expected to conform to high professional and ethical standards. Honesty, trustworthiness, and high moral conduct are essential leadership traits. Recent ethical problems among some of the nation's highest executives have prompted corporations to formulate new policies on the subject, while granting little tolerance.

Leaders tend to radiate energy. Whenever articles are written about America's top corporate leaders, a trait common to them all is the habit of arriving early at the office. Whether you are the head of a huge corporation, department, or section, it's smart to get into the office early because it conveys responsible leadership, which multiples throughout the organization. Leaders set the tone of every organization and provide the spirit needed to achieve new heights.

You can acquire leadership qualities. The fact that you are reading this book indicates that you have a genuine desire to strengthen your personal effectiveness and achieve leadership status.

The ability to manage people by leading rather than controlling is the sign of a true leader.

PLANNING FOR SUCCESS

Planning is a vital trait for every leader. In the business world, planning is probably the most important function of an enterprise. Good planners excel in defining problems and developing innovative solutions. They often confer with their assistants at the beginning of each day to review priorities, deadlines, and action plans. They establish priorities and prepare plans of action that are timely, realistic, and positive. They develop sound strategies and expect the best.

You want to demonstrate to your superiors that you are forward looking and would welcome an opportunity to participate in strategic planning.

Skilled planners display a calm and cool approach to their work. They are not in constant motion putting out fires.

Plan your activities so that you are managing your job rather than letting your job manage you.

In short, plan your work and work your plans.

ORGANIZING FOR RESULTS

Organizing is a critical function of management. Successful managers organize their responsibilities and activities to achieve the best results.

If you are in a management position, you should organize your division, department, or section in a manner that will place responsibility and decision making at the lowest possible level. Placing responsibility at the lowest level builds people and promotes a climate providing participation and opportunity. Be sure that you do not overstaff because people are more effective when they are busy and challenged.

The higher a person reports in an organization, the more satisfaction is generally experienced. Being close to the power base is exciting and generates a tremendous amount of enthusiasm, pride, and spirit.

A sales person would rather report to a regional sales manager than a zone manager. Executive secretaries often enjoy tremendous job satisfaction and security despite a salary that may be considerably lower than that of managers who report at much lower levels.

New office technologies are frequently breaking up jobs into lower-paid and less-challenging positions. Computerization in many organizations is contributing to greater employee regimentation. Effective managers structure jobs to include opportunities for discretion, creativity and challenge.

In a strong organization, lines of authority are clearly established. Despite the cases that are presented for matrix and other loose organizations, a one-on-one reporting relationship has stood the test of time.

RECOGNIZING THE VALUE OF POSITIONS DESCRIPTIONS

Since every company has both formal and informal organizational structures, it is important that new employees clearly understand their reporting relationships. Office politicians often make special efforts to assert authority over new employees, and a good manager will take measures to ensure that proper reporting is understood and followed.

Problems often arise whenever a person has a dual reporting relationship. Sometimes persons are assigned to one individual and also given a functional reporting relationship to another. For example, a game playing executive will select a preferred project and tell the other executive that the joint subordinate is working on a priority assignment that will require full-time attention.

Dual reporting does have job security benefits. You can be sure that the influence of two executives can keep most persons challenged and fully employed.

CONTROLLING COSTS

As cost containment achieves permanent status in the corporate culture, judgment becomes increasingly critical in the area of financial control. Responsible managers are trimming costs at every opportunity. They are striving to mold organizations that are truly "lean and mean."

Cost cutting should always be undertaken for the best interest of the organization and not personal gain. New executives have a tendency to promptly eliminate divisions, people, and products. For example, a company that has spent millions of dollars in developing a new product should not allow a new vice president to prematurely discontinue the line in order to gain personal recognition as a cost cutter.

MAKING BUDGETS WORK

Strong executives demonstrate responsible financial management. They develop budgets on the basis of actual need.

Although budgeting is a key management responsibility, it can become somewhat of a corporate game. Department managers will submit inflated budgets knowing that management will likely require reductions at a later date. When reductions are ordered, the already inflated budget will be cut, and the department will receive the monies that were desired in the first place.

The author is aware of many instances where companies place large orders at the end of the year. Department managers know that if they do not expend budgeted monies they are not likely to receive them again.

Once a budget is approved, you need to closely monitor it. Successful budgeting requires that prompt action be taken whenever major variances first begin to appear. If variances are not given prompt attention, they tend to become compounded and cannot be easily rectified.

Powerful executives make every effort to stay within assigned budgets. However, they do not view budgets as a straight jacket. If unforeseeable opportunities arise, strong managers request a special budget variance. Companies cannot afford to miss out on opportunities due to a weak executive who is obsessed with meeting the assigned budget.

Budgets provide an excellent opportunity to develop accountability. Keep in mind that responsibility and authority go together. Persons with responsibility must be given the monies needed to accomplish the expected results. Budgets should also be prepared at the lowest level in the organization to encourage participation and a sense of responsibility.

Subordinates are often denied a raise or other request because "it's not in the budget." Smart subordinates will learn the time of year when their superior is participating in preparing the annual budget. The best time to make a request is shortly before the budget is prepared.

If you have a budget, monitor it closely and make every effort to keep expenditures within allocated amounts. Be prepared to request special variances if significant and unexpected opportunities arise.

A failure to control cost is prime justification for termination. Costs involve numbers, and no one can dispute a well-documented history of cost failures.

MAKING BETTER DECISIONS

The ability to take decisive action is a key trait of every leader. Decision making can definitely be improved. A commonly taught technique is to write down the advantages and disadvantages of a decision. By assigning a point value to each factor, you can total the points to indicate the best course of action.

Another method for improving decision making involves practice. For example, if you pass a store window with three suits displayed, ask yourself which suit you would select. Repeated practice of this exercise will train you to become a better decision maker.

Secure executives gather all facts and ask staff input when making big decisions. Business is becoming so complex that an interdisciplinary approach in thinking is virtually essential.

If you are a supervisor, encourage subordinates to solve their problems and make their own decisions. For example, the story is told of the high school quarterback who was facing a fourth down and two situations in a very important game. The quarterback looked at the coach on the sideline for a play, but the coach merely looked down at the grass. The message was loud and clear—"I have confidence in you—Make your own decision."

Never take a problem to your superior without a proposed solution. Employee A, for example, may go to the boss and say, "Boy have we got a problem. XYZ Company refuses to accept our price increase. Where do we go from here?"

Employee B, on the other hand, may say, "Well, we have a problem. XYZ Company refuses to accept our price increase. Now, I have given the situation a lot of thought, and it seems to me that we have three options available:

1. We can hold the line and possibly lose the business;

2. We can provide them with a thorough cost analysis and demonstrate our need in greater detail; or

3. We can offer them a private brand at a lower cost.

Of the three options, I recommend that we pursue number three. Perhaps you can think of other options, or do you concur with pursuing option three?"

Managers find it very difficult to terminate an employee whom they have come to rely upon for solid advice in decision making. A trusted subordinate with good decision-making skills can greatly enhance job security.

Once a decision is made, you are obligated to give it your full support. Personal feelings must be set aside as you concentrate on successfully communicating and implementing the planned strategy. Decisions are not always right, but organizations must move in a unified direction.

Executives develop people by making them think. They make people grow by involving them in the decision-making process.

In general, first impressions are the best and timing is critical. Also, if in doubt . . . don't.

Concerns about job security are turning many managers into weak executives. Managers often become ultraconservative wimps who are afraid to take any course of action that carries risk. They are more concerned about preserving their jobs and the status quo. They often procrastinate and become dead wood to the company.

At a time when many firms are fighting for survival, companies need innovative employees who are willing to take risks and move their organizations forward.

People who risk nothing, have nothing!

EXERCISING SOUND JUDGMENT

A person with good judgment has the ability to effectively diagnose situations and conditions. He or she displays an ability to think, reason, and take appropriate action to solve problems. Intuitive judgment is based on an inner feeling influenced by education, experience, and training.

Because organizations tend to be political institutions, you need to always make sure that your judgments are based on facts.

Good judgment requires that you obtain the best possible input when considering a strategy. Do not hesitate to gather opinions from co-workers and other staff personnel. Secretaries often possess outstanding intuitive judgment and can often provide different viewpoints to consider.

Avoid making quick decisions. Keep an open mind and weigh all alternative action plans. Try not to be governed by conventional wisdom and thoroughly consider all options in terms of consequences. Always consider ethical and moral grounds. A person with good judgment strengthens job security and is valuable to every organization.

DEVELOPING COMPETENCY

Competency reflects ability and professionalism. Competency is acquired by education, training, experience and dedication. Your ability to develop competency is essential to your job security.

People value competency and professionalism. If you have a leaking roof, you want a roofer who knows his or her stuff. When you take your car to a mechanic, you want someone that can diagnosis the problem and fix it with no ifs, ands, or buts.

Competent persons are often highly trained and dedicated. They strive for perfection and develop skills that meet the highest standards of professional excellence. Experience is a major factor contributing to the development of competency. Would you rather go to a heart surgeon who only performs several operations a year or one who performs many?

In addition to being competent, you need to convey it. Competency builds respect, trust, and confidence. Develop a reputation for having strong confidence in yourself.

DEMONSTRATING CREATIVITY

A creative person is innovative and imaginative. Creative people are continuously exploring new approaches, concepts, and techniques. They are willing to experiment and welcome new ideas at every opportunity. One idea can be more rewarding than a lifetime of working.

As humans, we tap very little of our creative potential. You can become more creative by changing your routine thinking and lifestyle. For example, you can take different routes to work, try new restaurants, and develop broader interests. Many schools, museums, and communities offer special-interest courses that can be very rewarding. In addition, it's important to seek creative approaches, innovative planning, and stimulating ideas. Also take a fresh new look toward your job.

Managers too frequently devote their energies to achieving immediate and tangible results. They become totally committed to processing paper, writing reports, and meeting deadlines. Managers must recognize that generating ideas is an inherent job responsibility and warrants sufficient time and effort.

People will submit more ideas in a supportive work environment. You can develop a creative work climate by promoting a sense of inquiry and encouraging the flow of fresh ideas.

Group brainstorming is an excellent technique for stimulating ideas. In brainstorming sessions, you should never criticize ideas no matter how bizarre they may appear.

Some people have a tendency to always criticize or take a negative position on any idea (particularly in meetings). People who criticize are frequently attempting to compensate for various personal weaknesses. They get satisfaction by putting other people down.

Effective managers display appreciation for all ideas and give proper recognition at every opportunity.

DISPLAYING TACT AND DIPLOMACY

Managers who display tact and diplomacy do and say the right thing at the right time. They handle situations with poise and understanding and take appropriate action without offending. They display good etiquette and follow proper protocol.

Tact denotes class and is highly valued in organizational life. Every firm has certain standards of conduct and protocol. For example, it is not courteous to barge into an office while a person is talking on the telephone.

Tactful and diplomatic managers show appreciation and convey congratulations at every opportunity. They send personal notes and cards on birthdays, anniversaries, promotions, retirements, etc.

Sales managers, for example, build goodwill by sending personal notes welcoming new customers and expressing appreciation for a large order. A business anniversary offers an excellent opportunity to convey appreciation for past business while providing assurance of continued support. A personal note of congratulations to a salesperson in recognition of a worthy accomplishment is tactful and reflects good business.

In today's bureaucratic and computerized world, the handwritten note has taken on a new meaning. A handwritten note is a sign of real class. While any executive can send a neatly typed communication, a handwritten note conveys sincerity. The habit of writing personal notes can be very effective and will build goodwill and many friendships.

In the business world, form letters are the only practical means of communicating with a large number of customers, clients, etc. The letter usually begins with a salutation such as "Dear valued customer" or something similar. Tactful executives will write on top of the salutation the first name of the recipient along with a note such as "Thanks so much for your business during the past year" and then sign their first name.

Worthy of special mention is the ability to recall names. Calling an individual by name reflects sincerity and tact. When meeting a person for the first time, always repeat his or her name aloud as it will help your future recall. Whenever you are introduced to a new person, remember to look into their eyes and extend a reasonably firm handshake.

If you are in doubt about whether to call a senior person by first name, it's best to remain formal until requested otherwise. Also, if you forget a person's name, it's best to ask the individual again.

BUILDING EMPLOYEE RAPPORT

A common trait of successful executives is their warm and genuine interest in the lives and welfare of company employees. Top managers always find time to be friendly and gracious with no regard to class or status. They extend first name greetings to everyone from the doorman to the chairman of the board. Simply put, they have style.

Job security is increased whenever an executive enjoys widespread popularity throughout an entire organization. Compare the following identical-level executives:

Executive A (old school)	Executive B (new school)
Keeps a closed-door policy	Maintains an open-door policy
Eats only in the executive dining room	Eats with different employees every day in the company cafeteria
Outside dining is only at a country or city club	Outside dining is at popular restaurants where employees are often seen
Knows very few employees	Knows a large number of employees by first name including security guards and mailroom clerks

Of the above executives, which one would you prefer to work for? Senior management can be very reluctant to jeopardize morale by terminating an employee who is extremely well liked in all areas of the company.

A smart manager shows respect for all employees and makes a strong effort to build rapport.

ENCOURAGING
DELEGATION

Top managers strive to bring out the best in people and maximize individual abilities. Real managers inspire a spirit of participation, teamwork, and achievement. They give credit to their subordinates and let them establish their own identity. They build on employee strengths and do not hesitate to delegate. They concentrate on the big picture and let subordinates handle administrative staff work and details.

Professional managers delegate to develop subordinates for promotion within the organization. They are people oriented and derive tremendous satisfaction from seeing subordinates rise to new heights.

Nothing is more discouraging to conscientious employees than a company that brings in a new person from the outside to fill a position that could have been given to a capable worker within the organization.

A growing number of companies are abandoning a long-established tradition by going outside the firm to fill key positions. Companies are searching for new ideas and fresh thinking.

If a company needs a nuclear physicist, it is understandable that there may not be a qualified person within the firm. However, going outside to fill a general administration position reflects poor management training and a total lack of human resources development. Passing qualified internal employees is demoralizing and certainly does not promote job security.

As more companies in America become consolidated, there will be a corresponding lack of employee growth opportunities. Employees are becoming increasingly slotted in jobs that offer little promotional opportunities. Persons who become stagnated often lose the driving spirit that is needed to make important contributions to their jobs, and as a result the entire organization suffers.

If you are in a supervisory position, you should make a strong effort to prevent employee stagnation. Measures that help to avoid stagnation include rotating employees into different jobs and increasing individual responsibilities.

Effective supervisors encourage active involvement. They keep jobs challenging and motivate employees to achieve personal and organizational goals.

Secretaries and administrative assistants are often underutilized and capable of making greater contributions. Office automation is dramatically increasing the efficiency of secretaries, making more time available for assignments that offer greater challenges. Top managers develop teamwork effectiveness and provide secretaries with interesting and challenging responsibilities.

TURNING VACATIONS INTO OPPORTUNITIES

Vacations play an important role in building greater job security. Smart employees never take a vacation during the same time as their boss. Although you may feel that you and your boss are an important team, others may not perceive it in the same light. If you are totally dependent on your superior, you may also lose your job should your boss be terminated.

Whenever a superior is on vacation, you have an excellent opportunity to prove your worth. You want to ask if you may assume greater responsibilities during your superior's absence. A good boss will make it known that you should be contacted if any problems arise in his or her absence.

A manager who returns from vacation will be very impressed with subordinates who have kept operations running smoothly. Many executives will take more and lengthier vacations when they know that trusted and capable subordinates can takeover. Your job security is strongly reinforced whenever you are providing essential backup.

You want to demonstrate that your education and experience have given you the confidence needed to successfully complete any task and deliver results on time. Build an image of being an action person who can get the job done in the absence of your superior.

Job security demands that you make your supportive services well known.

MAXIMIZING TITLES

Assigning better titles to subordinates makes it easier for them to handle delegation. The world is impressed with titles. Have you ever noticed how many vice presidents are employed by advertising agencies, stockbrokers, and banks? Titles convey authority and gain respect.

When asked what they do, people without titles typically say that they work for XYZ Company. How much better it is to say that you are a marketing specialist or special projects coordinator for the XYZ Company?

Titles build self-esteem and make people feel good about themselves and their jobs. People who enjoy their jobs speak well about their employer and convey positive attitudes to the all-important customer.

If you are ever denied a promotion, ask for a better title. Keep in mind that titles strengthen your resume.

Good managers upgrade titles at every deserving opportunity. The position of sales person is being widely replaced by district or territory manager, etc. Secretaries are becoming executive assistants or administrative assistants.

DELEGATING PITFALLS

A factor discouraging delegation and the development of subordinates is the growing insecurity of middle management. Some managers are so concerned about protecting their own turf that they cannot delegate. They are afraid that management will recognize that their subordinates can capably handle their jobs at a much lower pay level.

Managers also frequently fail to delegate because of a number of other factors including the following:

1. A lack of professional trust in subordinates
2. A fear that control will be lost
3. A feeling that "doing" is the only means of proving one's worth
4. A belief that "doing" provides the only way of getting things done right
5. A perception that only "doing" provides personal satisfaction

To delegate effectively, you must clearly define the duties involved and the objective to be achieved. If you wish to make persons accountable, you must give them the authority needed to carry out the delegated responsibility. It is also important that you inform others of the delegated responsibility in order to gain their cooperation and support.

Many managers do not delegate because of their high energy level. They must be in constant motion and often by-pass or ignore subordinates. Over a period of time, these executives fail to develop people and can seriously weaken an organization.

It is always pathetic to see nondelegators putting in long hours while their subordinates maintain reasonable work schedules and life styles. Clearly, the nondelegator has no place in modern management and is ripe for replacement.

You can evaluate the ability to delegate by observing the operation of a department or group in the absence of the person in charge. If a department virtually shuts down when the manager is not present, you can be sure that little delegation has taken place. Conversely, the continued smooth operation in the absence of the manager reflects strong delegation and the development of competent subordinates.

Whenever you delegate, you continue to assume ultimate responsibility. Strong executives also give full support to their subordinates especially when the going gets tough. You should never undercut your subordinates. A sales person, for example, may call on a customer for years without a problem. If a serious problem arises, the president or a vice president may call on higher levels of the account without inviting the local representative to participate. Actions of this type seriously undermine the image of an assigned representative and certainly do not build confidence or respect.

Delegating the authority to issue approvals is a powerful technique for increasing efficiency and developing subordinates. Top executives delegate approval authorizations because they have developed a trust in employees. They recognize that employees who are closest to any situation are in the best position to make decisions and give approvals within predetermined limits.

Sometimes approvals can be so cumbersome that vice presidents may be required to approve a personnel form listing the change of an employee name because of marriage. In effect, the company is approving the marriage!

Approvals should be authorized at the lowest possible level. All approvals involving large expenditures should always require the signature of two persons regardless of the level.

The ability to delegate approval authority is largely determined by the caliber of your subordinates. Consequently, you want to hire the best people who are capable, ambitious and desire greater responsibility.

Some managers have the misguided impression that they can best maintain their positions of power by hiring weak subordinates. Nothing could be further from the truth. Whenever the need arises, you want to hire the most qualified candidate that you can find. Hiring capable people will ultimately strengthen your effectiveness and benefit the entire company.

Security-minded employees make a special effort to work for a person who is known as a strong delegator. It's simply smart to occasionally offer to relieve your superior of any duties that you can capably perform. Assuming increased duties that were previously performed by your boss is a great job security builder.

Remember the neatest and most orderly desks are normally found at the top level of any organization.

INCREASING JOB
SECURITY WITH
KNOWLEDGE

Knowledge runs an organization and successful persons are exceptionally well informed. You need to thoroughly know your job, your organization, and your industry or field. It's especially important that you know how your function fits into the bigger picture.

The world of business is changing at such a fast pace that you must keep informed to protect the interests of yourself and your employer. Areas such as employment and taxation, for example, are undergoing continuous change due to new laws, regulations, and guidelines. By keeping informed, you can effectively handle responsibility in an environment with greater risks for both personal and corporate liability.

Make every effort to keep on the cutting edge of all developments in your field. You want to develop a situation where your employer is depending on you to keep up with the very latest developments that are occurring in every job area.

The world is becoming smaller with a growing need for a global perspective. Individuals concerned about job security in the business world will find it advisable to expand their knowledge of global activities such as balance of trade, import and export activities, foreign currency rates, etc. International trade promises to be a strong career path for college students of today.

American corporations are increasingly looking overseas for growth markets. International manufacturing and marketing offers great long-term opportunities for job security. Persons who are fluent in foreign languages are especially in strong demand.

Ambitious persons will also benefit by joining trade and professional associations that relate to their chosen field. Active involvement in professional groups will build personal contacts, keep you on top of your field, and provide opportunities for increasing your visibility.

Contacts made through professional associations can be especially valuable when looking for a new job. Networking is a good insurance policy.

Trade and professional associations often maintain vast information resources. Make a special effort to read association bulletins and monitor the activities of all firms in your industry or field.

Subscribe to numerous publications in your field and route articles of special interest to others for their information. Ask to have your name placed on routing slips.

It's also valuable to periodically attend seminars, symposiums, lectures, etc. After you attend a meeting, always send your superior a brief report of the conference and describe how you plan to apply the new knowledge to improve your job performance.

Even if you are refused permission to attend a seminar because of cost or some other reason, you have made it known that you are ready, willing, and eager to develop yourself for advancement.

You can greatly increase your job security by learning new skills. Examples of skills that you can acquire are speed-reading, creative writing, improved memory, speech making, and foreign languages.

Many employers pay part or all of an employee's tuition fees. The opportunity to become better educated and improve advancement potential at your employer's expense is a winning combination. If available, take advantage of all employer tuition programs.

Assume you are the manager of an international order department. You have a number of order processors working for you. One of your subordinates requests your approval to participate in the company's paid tuition program. You approve the request and the employee enters a night course at a local university to learn French.

Several months later, the company announces a retrenchment program and the order department manager is told to eliminate one employee. Do you really believe the person studying French is going to be terminated? No way! Improving specialized job skills is one of your best strategies for a more secure future.

You should acquire a strong working knowledge of computers because they have dramatically changed organizational life. The time spent in improving your computer skills is a solid investment in your job security.

If a publicly owned corporation employs you, it's good practice to purchase a few shares of the company's stock. By receiving quarterly and annual reports, you can become knowledgeable about the company and keep informed of management trends, directions, and strategies.

You can also obtain helpful information about your employer by developing friendships with employees who are assigned to entirely different areas of the company. By scheduling occasional coffee breaks with persons outside your area, you will be amazed at the new and different insights that can be shared on common issues.

For many years, the author took coffee breaks with a group of executives representing many departments of a large international corporation. The breaks took place in the corner of a large company cafeteria with hundreds of other employees. The group gained a reputation for being so knowledgeable that one of the company's highest executives would often join the table just to learn what was going on.

The interchange of information was actually of benefit to the firm. Sometimes it seemed that the "informal board" had a better understanding of company developments than the real board of directors.

One of the most common weaknesses of executives is that they become aloof from the realities of the business world. Years of street smarts may have helped them advance to very high levels at corporate headquarters. As the years go by, they lose touch with the real world.

If they have a problem with their company car, they merely call the garage and request that it be taken to the dealer for service while a loaner is provided for the trip home. They cannot relate to the average person who finds that being without a car is almost a catastrophic experience. After all, who will take the sick child to the doctor tomorrow?

If you are in sales management, you need to stay in touch with your customers by periodically making calls at all levels of distribution. Many retail executives make a commitment to periodically visit their stores. You can talk to your front-line managers and customers to learn about their problems, successes, and opportunities.

Some of the most secure and knowledgeable persons in any business are the star sales performers. In the advent of a takeover, sales forces are often merged and many persons are terminated. You can be sure that top sales achievers will survive because they are the big contributors to the bottom line.

In many companies, customer complaints are usually handled by low level people. Since customers are the lifeblood of a company, serious product complaints should be handled at a relatively high level by managers who have the authority to make corrections.

In the manufacturing area, executives can make periodic visits to outlying plants in order to get a better understanding of floor operations, quality problems, and worker attitudes.

Corporations run on positive attitudes. Problems occur when the desire to be positive obscures reality. Executives can surround themselves with so many positive but unrealistic thinkers that they soon enter a make believe world.

Going direct to the front lines cuts through the bureaucracy and provides the type of solid information than can be used to make hard decisions.

In addition to keeping in touch with business operations, successful executives maintain a network of personal contacts. Modern day communications make it easy to maintain friendships with old college chums, military acquaintances, former co-workers, and others.

Many executives devote considerable time and effort to contact old friends during the holiday season. Some people even prepare and send a holiday newsletter to their friends.

The days of devoting a career to one employer are long gone, making a network of personal contacts more important than ever. Remember that your best job security is your employability, and keeping your contacts alive is critical. Staying in touch with both professional and personal friends is a wise investment for the present and future.

DEALING WITH CLIQUES

Cliques will invariably form in every organization. They are normally comprised of individuals with common backgrounds or interests. A clique may involve all persons who formerly operated a certain plant or were promoted from the same geographic area. Sometimes persons hired during a certain period form cliques.

Cliques often become a very powerful force and may even surpass the official organization as an information gathering source and communications center. Cliques can sometimes accomplish an objective that would be very difficult for the organization to handle.

Smart executives keep very much aware of cliques. Additionally, top managers recognize that cliques can be very demoralizing to nonmembers, and they take measure to ensure that all employees are given equal consideration on the basis of performance, not association.

The acquisition of knowledge is a prerequisite to effective performance and job security.

COMMUNICATING FOR GREATER JOB SECURITY

In today's shrinking world, communication skills are becoming increasingly important to achieving job security. The growth of video tape, optical cables, satellite communications, and other electronic means places a high premium on the ability to communicate.

It is vital that you maintain open communication with your superiors, subordinates, and co-workers. A top priority is to keep your superiors informed of your activities. You can maintain open communication by sending simple "for your information" e-mails. Superiors who are kept informed are more likely to support you and provide guidance for your mutual gain.

How you communicate is often as important as what you communicate. Your communications should be short, frank, sincere, and truthful.

By the same token, listening is crucial to effective communications. You need to encourage an interchange of ideas, develop a sense of inquiry, and display conversational tact.

Listening is especially critical in the interviewing process. If you are seeking a job, try to let the interviewer do much of the talking. Some interviewers will use the discussion to reinforce their ego. They will go on and on in discussing the greatness of the company, its products, future, etc. In effect, the interviewer is saying that he or she is really somebody because they are employed by such a fantastic company. In so doing, the person will transfer his or her positive feelings to your evaluation.

If you are the interviewer, you should follow a semi-structured interview pattern and encourage the applicant to talk about two-thirds of the time. By adhering to a semi-structured interview, you treat all applicants equally and can develop more objective evaluations.

One of the habits to avoid in an organization is the "closed-door syndrome." The mere closing of a door seems to give some managers a real feeling of power. In some organizations, closed doors are much more common in middle management than in top management.

Closed doors are interpreted as a danger signal in many companies. Envision a scene where the human resources director enters the office of a vice president who immediately shuts the door. The news will spread like wildfire in a highly visible office. Telephones will begin ringing throughout the organization, and everyone will start to wonder what is happening.

As organizational life becomes more competitive in slow-growth or no-growth companies, communications with employees take on greater importance. In times of job insecurity, people tend to talk more. Rumors become more frequent and usually more accurate.

In the absence of a formal communication program, employees develop their own communication network. A closely knit group of secretaries, telephone operators, and mail room clerks can often be extremely well informed. An employee communication network in a negative mode can be devastating to an organization.

COMMUNICATING CORPORATE DEVELOPMENTS

House organs, if properly edited, can provide an excellent opportunity to communicate with employees. Unfortunately, house organs too often feature profiles of management members that turn the publication into an "ego press."

Also, managements often believe that a house organ featuring "babies and bowling" fulfills their communications responsibility. The fact is that today's employees want to read more than news of service recognitions or social events. They want to know about the company, its profitability, and direction.

Management communications should reflect integrity, credibility, and honesty. A common danger is the use of puffery. For example, a company will send a letter to employees stating, "We are pleased to announce a new benefits program." Since the new program includes higher and costlier co-payments, employees wonder why the company is so pleased to make the announcement.

Corporate writers have a tendency to prepare flow-ery statements that will be well accepted by upper management. In striving to please management, puffery can easily replace accuracy.

Whenever decisions are reached that affect employ-ees, strong managements immediately release the news. A straightforward management communica-tions program reduces organizational tension and builds sincerity and credibility.

At one time it was common practice for companies to announce bad news on Friday. It was thought that the weekend would give employees time to digest the news and prevent an opportunity to con-fer with other employees.

Today, more and more executives believe that it is better to announce bad news early in the week. In times of stress, employees have a need to discuss the situation with superiors, subordinates, and peers. Announcing distressing news early in the week con-veys the impression of a sincere management, in con-trast to late Friday announcements that can often be construed as management cop-outs.

Increased publicity is making corporations more sensitive to verbal and written communications. The ability to convey factual information to the commu-nity in a manner that will reflect as favorably as pos-sible on the organization is of growing importance.

The nation's media is giving greater attention to the reporting of business news. Companies are responding with carefully worded communications aimed at a highly selected audience. In general, companies send different messages to the finan-cial community, unions, and employees.

It is always interesting to compare employee commu-nications with a company's annual report. In a tone of gloom and doom, employees may be told that poor business conditions will require layoffs, plant closings, etc. The annual report will cover the same subject in a very positive manner. The statement concerning poor business conditions will be changed to "In keeping with our corporate strategy of positioning ourselves for greater earnings, we are . . ."

Your communications convey a favorable or unfavorable image for your employer. Strive to give an impression that projects a positive and accurate image of your organization, its products, or services. As long as you are on the payroll, you have an obligation to speak well of your employer.

Keep attuned to the organizational grapevine but do not become directly involved in gossip because it can be detrimental to your career. Likewise, it's best to avoid discussions involving religion and politics.

Emphasize the positive and be the bearer of good news at every opportunity.

IMPROVING ORAL EXPRESSION

Persons who excel in oral expression possess a very powerful trait in organizational life. They display an ability to present views logically and make presentations with poise and confidence. They excel in impromptu speaking and are very persuasive. They speak in a positive tone and are very articulate.

You can definitely improve your speaking ability. However, the only way to really become an effective speaker is to acquire actual experience.

You can read many valuable books on the subject but there simply is not any substitute for real experience.

You can steadily develop your confidence by speaking at every opportunity. Offer to say a few words at retirement parties, celebrations, and other events of your organization and community.

Prior to speaking, you can develop a feeling of positive emotions by thinking of your major successes and accomplishments. It's also good practice to personally meet members of an audience before delivering a speech. Establishing a friendly atmosphere creates an environment of trust and helps put you at ease.

Based on considerable experience as a speech writer, it is the author's belief that every speaker should have a prepared outline or complete text for all formal talks. The knowledge that material is available for immediate reference provides confidence and self-assurance. In addition, many executives have a tendency to become cute or clever at the podium, and they may make passing remarks that are later regretted. An outline or text keeps speakers on track.

Humor in speech making should be used with extreme caution. Speakers may test jokes on co-workers and secretaries with great success only to encounter a cool response before a real audience. If in doubt about using humor in a speech, don't.

Today, it's also easy to offend different factions of any audience. While divergent views cannot always be avoided, you want to gain a positive response from your total audience. Special attention should be given to any reference to race, religion, sex, nationality, and politics.

In situations where you are called upon to say a few remarks, you can excel by following a very simple formula that applies to all situations. The formula is to simply say a few words about the past, present, and future. For example, "I can remember when this group had only 18 members and today we have 50 members and we will no doubt reach 100 members within a few years."

Another helpful tip is to first say to yourself whatever you wish to say to a group and then stand up and say it aloud.

Strong oral expression warrants a high priority to persons seeking greater job security.

IMPROVING YOUR WRITING ABILITY

The ability to write clearly and effectively is vital to your success. The key to successful writing is to keep it short and simple. One page letters pack the greatest punch. If it's necessary to write a number of pages, summarize the report or message in a single page.

Whenever subordinates prepare a report, it's a good management practice to distribute the report over the signature of the person who prepared it. Personalization builds people, pride, and accountability.

Keep your writing positive. Avoid complaining or expressing job dissatisfaction in writing, because you may later regret it. Negative communications frequently surface under entirely different circumstances, such as under a new superior, and one outburst of emotion in writing can have a long-term negative impact on your job security.

Write to communicate rather than to impress.

MANAGING TIME

Successful people have learned to effectively manage time. They excel in setting priorities and concentrate on those activities that yield the biggest payoff. They schedule all appointments, eliminate unnecessary paperwork, and maintain control over interruptions.

Smart managers place a high value on time. They are not willing to spend hours in idle conversation or sit in unproductive meetings that drag on forever. Time-conscientious persons stay in control of their activities. They run their jobs rather than let their jobs run them.

CONTROLLING MEETINGS

Busy nonachievers are strong proponents of meetings. Despite the best efforts of a well-meaning chairperson, meetings too frequently serve the purpose of a ritual rather than an effective group effort. Meetings commonly fail to accomplish results, and they provide a supposedly legitimate opportunity for nonachievers to waste their own time as well as the valuable time of others.

A series of meetings scheduled for the same time will become so routine that effectiveness is soon lost. Before long, it will be time for a meeting because it's Tuesday!

Indecisive managers are especially fond of meetings because they make it possible to transfer responsibility for tough decisions or unpopular decisions to a group. It's easier to blame a group with well-recorded minutes for a bad decision than to accept personal responsibility.

Meetings also provide an opportunity to escape from ringing telephones and decision-making tasks. Management by frequent meetings reflects the lack of a strong organization that has clearly- defined job responsibilities and decisive leadership.

Persons who are always in staff meetings can project a very negative image. Customers and clients become disgusted when the person they are trying to contact is always in a meeting. It's a short-sighted organization that gives a higher priority to internal meetings than to the people who support their very existence.

Action people schedule meetings sparely but make them count.

SCHEDULING TIME

Business travel is another area providing tremendous potential for improved time savings. Travel too often serves the psychological purpose of reinforcing an executive's career level. Seeing the country or world and eating in the best restaurants at company expense is an opportunity that might otherwise not be possible.

Using telephones and telephone conferencing are logical alternatives to travel. In today's cost-conscious world, the efficient use of electronic communications in lieu of travel is essential.

Arriving at the office before normal working hours provides a quiet time that many find to be the most productive time of the day. The period before the opening of a busy office offers an opportunity to plan the day's activities and is especially useful for doing creative work.

Many persons perform at peak efficiency during the early morning hours. It is usually best to schedule brainwork in the morning along with important activities. In the afternoon, business activity often slows and people begin planning for the next day.

In addition to arriving early at the office, it's generally smart to often stay after closing time. You do not want to become known as a clock-watcher. Some persons arrive early at the office, take extra-long lunches, and then stay late to show their dedication!

More importantly, the atmosphere in many offices tends to become more relaxed and informal after the scheduled closing hours. Opportunities for communicating with top executives that would be virtually impossible during the day often become available after hours.

Many strong relationships with high-level executives have been developed after hours. In times of a job crisis, these relationships may become of extreme value.

Top performers also plan their most important activities for early in the week. People are refreshed from the weekend and are more motivated to achieve results.

Weeks in the business world often get off to a fast start. Airports can be extremely busy on Sunday evenings. Incoming mail and other communications are often the heaviest on Mondays. Business operations tend to slow as holidays and weekends approach.

Holiday weeks for most businesses tend to be very slow. More and more employees are scheduling vacations that include holidays. It is often difficult to contact others during a holiday week, and major projects often come to a standstill.

A common myth is the tendency to believe that you must be continuously busy to be effective. Frequently, it is the insecure manager who feels compelled to be extremely busy at all times.

Action managers delegate to achieve time effectiveness. They keep things simple and make effective use of secretarial and other support. Ambitious persons who are fortunate to work for action people are generally happy and grow rapidly in their careers.

To achieve the greatest time effectiveness, you want to maximize your peak times periods and concentrate on the 20 percent of your job that normally produces 80 percent of the significant results. Try to work smarter, not harder.

Don't confuse activity with accomplishment.

Keeping Up with Technology

Improving Administrative Effectiveness

To be a strong administrator, you need to continuously develop improved systems and procedures. You need to keep well informed of the latest developments in office administration and install the most efficient systems for communicating and retrieving information.

Computerization now permits top management to directly assess virtually all electronically processed information. Administrative effectiveness is becoming increasingly dependent on your ability to manage computer-generated information. Obviously, if you want job security in administration, you need to become proficient in computer information processing.

A situation that often occurs is "computer dependency." Many executives have the simplistic impression that computers are the means for solving all problems.

Phrases such as "let the computer do it" are frequently heard in the office environment. The problem is that information must first be fed into a computer. Many seem to believe that computers are purchased with the company's data already programmed, and merely flicking a switch will give you an instant print-out of any conceivable information.

The fact is that it takes some good thinking and a lot of time to program and enter meaningful information into a computer. Additionally, data must continuously be fed into a computer in order to maintain current information.

A problem that frequently occurs is the tendency of organizations to purchase personal computers without giving sufficient attention to software requirements and training. Without appropriate programs and training, computers can quickly become under-utilized.

Professional administrators make every effort to reduce paperwork rather than increase it. Not too long ago, it was predicted that computers would create a paperless office. Experience has shown that electronic information is too often increasing paperwork.

As office employees become more familiar with computers, there is a tendency to produce more reports. Information that was once typed in alphabetical order is soon listed by date, state, quantity, etc. Before you know it, high-speed printers are continuously grinding out data that is measured in depth by the foot.

Sometimes a purchase order for a single book will comprise several feet of pages. You would think a nuclear submarine were being ordered.

In addition, paper reports require filing. Storing information electronically is certainly cheaper and more efficient.

An auditor recently told the author that many small businesses keep their records on both computers and paper. They simply are not comfortable using computers as the sole source for vital information.

Unfortunately, organizational people like paper documents. Paper can be shuffled, stapled, reviewed, noted, approved, revised, highlighted, etc. It can be piled on desks to convey the impression that one is extremely busy. It can be carried in binders, notebooks, and attaché cases. If you take paperwork away from many executives, they become totally frustrated and helpless.

Despite the fondness for paper, the best method of improving the operating efficiency of any office is to create electronic documents more efficiently and get them to the people who have a functional need to see them. Electronically processed information is the key to improving office productivity.

Effective administrators keep things simple. They are results oriented rather than paper oriented. They avoid duplication of effort and attempt to keep the number of persons handling documents to a minimum. They do not burden management with administrative details but use reporting by exception to keep superiors informed of major trends and developments.

The business world is becoming more electronically dependent, and companies are very reluctant to

terminate employees who excel in vital areas of electronic administration.

DISPLAYING ETHICS AND LOYALTY

Ethical behavior relates to what is acceptable or unacceptable . . . or is it simply what is right? Sometimes business people face tough decisions as to whether they should compromise personal values and principles in order to attain corporate goals.

In recent years, corporate behavior has attracted much publicity. Major ethical problems among some of the nation's top executives have received tremendous attention. Ethical issues are now being given greater attention in all business considerations and in new "codes of ethics."

Ethical considerations arise everyday in business ranging from small to large issues.

Is it right to take pencils home from work?

Is it right for a company to announce a new lower price on a product when the container size and contents are smaller?

> Is it right for cruise lines to advertise a cruise price at a very low level and then charge for virtually every service onboard?

> Is it right for companies to have signs posted at large copy machines warning employees that copyrighted material is not to be reproduced under any circumstances, while copies of copyrighted newsletters appear throughout the office?

> Is it right for companies to report higher earnings based on financial manipulations rather than true revenues and profits?

Often there is a fine line between ethical and legal matters. Nevertheless, there are many gray areas, and you always protect your job security by doing what is truly right.

SETTING REALISTIC AND HONEST OBJECTIVES

Nearly every position requires that you set some type of objective. Ethical problems often arise because objectives are made in an environment that is filled with enthusiasm, emotion, and pressures to excel. Sales managers want to forecast higher sales, financial people want higher earnings, and manufacturing executives want higher quality and output. Shareholders want better quarterly results.

Unrealistic objectives can cause serious company problems and negatively affect a career. Unrealistic projections are picked up by financial analysts and can often place a company in a defensive position.

For example, a vice-president of sales will announce at the company's annual meeting that the goal is to achieve a 10 percent increase in sales for the coming year. Manufacturing, in turn, plans production and inventories to meet the expected demand. The 10 percent figure is given excellent coverage in the company's house organ and press. Ten months later, a financial analyst calls the chief executive officer and says, "Mr. Jones, your company reported earlier in the year that your sales goal is to attain a 10 percent increase. Through nine months, your sales are up only 3.8 percent. Will you please comment on the reasons why you are substantially behind your goal?"

The CEO will come up with all kinds of excuses such as the weather, government regulations, foreign competition, etc.

At this point the CEO is furious because of the vice president's emotion-packed projection. The fact that the CEO was given a draft of the speech and never commented on the 10 percent increase is overlooked and irrelevant.

If the goal had been set at 3.5 percent, the current 3.8 percent achievement would be positive news because the goal was not only met but surpassed.

If you truly believe that the amount of overtime can be reduced 5 percent, it's not smart to inform your management that a 10 percent decrease will be achieved. Instead, establish a 4 percent objective. If the 5 percent is achieved, you have exceeded your goal and are to be complimented.

Many top executives have lost their jobs because of an inability to reach publicly announced goals.

Nonethical behavior is a sure ticket to the unemployment office. When faced with a decision, ask yourself if this is the ethical or the decent thing to do?

You can develop creditability by always establishing realistic goals. A balance between optimism and realism is the key.

CONVEYING LOYALTY AND DEDICATION

Loyalty is devotion to a duty or a cause. Persons who first enter organizational life often feel that loyalty is limited to giving so many hours of work in return for a paycheck. If you want to succeed, you should develop a high self-esteem, take pride in your work, and consider yourself to be a very important member of the team.

Whenever leaders are polled to learn of the traits that they consider most valued in subordinates, loyalty and dedication almost always appear high on the list. Loyalty is a most respected trait and is often given priority over technical skills when persons are chosen for retention.

You want to be loyal to yourself, your profession, organization, superiors, and subordinates. Whenever the going gets tough, you should back your superiors and subordinates with your fullest support.

Loyalty to yourself is critical. If you are misled, manipulated, or given unjust treatment, you should make every effort to openly discuss the situation with your superior. If all efforts fail, the best trade-off is to seek a transfer or a position elsewhere.

Loyalty in American organizations is undergoing a tremendous change. Many employees believe that they are only loyal until their next paycheck.

In competing for world markets, managements are under growing pressure to produce earnings. As top management turnover increases, each new CEO has one mission—add to the bottom line. Despite carefully worded statements, new CEOs often have little loyalty to existing employees. The point is reinforced whenever a new CEO brings in former associates while making cutbacks in long-term employees.

Although personnel retrenchment programs are often necessary due to unforeseen circumstances, they too frequently reflect a lack of long-range management planning and not only destroy loyalty but unfortunately contribute to a low public esteem of business.

The anxieties and strains resulting from restructuring and the loss of jobs can have a devastating impact on a person's well-being. Severe pressures can be placed on finances and families.

Many organizational observers believe that a growing number of companies no longer want employee loyalty. They are of the opinion that companies simply do not want to assume the responsibilities that go with loyalty such as fully-funded pension plans.

Loyalty is a two-way street. Organizations that expect loyalty must also give loyalty.

The loyalty that was once given to an organization is increasingly directed to personal goals or to a profession. The new loyalty has propelled a rapid growth in the self-help field.

In a corporate environment characterized by insecurity and uncertainty, personal initiative becomes of critical importance. Dedicated employees can no longer rely on employers to provide long-term job security. As a result, a growing number of employees are looking to government, schools, and other essential services for greater job security.

If you are going to be a successful and secure employee, you must act like one, and that requires loyalty to yourself and your profession.

REALIZING THE IMPORTANCE OF PERFORMANCE APPRAISALS

A prime responsibility of every person in a supervisory position is the evaluation of employee performance. Most organizations formally appraise performance at least once a year. The evaluation process enables an organization to take an inventory of human resources and provide information for personnel development and salary administration.

The appraisal program too often becomes a mechanical procedure with managers more concerned about filling out forms in order to meet deadlines imposed by the human resources department. Additionally, performance appraisals are frequently used to justify salary increases rather then rate true job performance.

Nevertheless, performance reviews take on new meaning whenever companies become distressed. In the advent of a discrimination lawsuit, performance appraisals are the first to be subpoenaed.

If you strongly disagree with a review, be sure to put your comments in writing, preferably on the form itself. It is absolutely essential that performance appraisals be used to accurately evaluate actual performance.

It is relatively easy to evaluate the performance of sales personnel in terms of volume. Production may be evaluated on the basis of output and quality. However, the performance of managerial, administrative, and clerical employees is much more difficult.

AVOIDING NEGATIVE NUMERICAL DOCUMENTATIONS

In the eighties, companies did not have very sophisticated strategies for winning employment discrimination lawsuits. During the nineties, they became experts in defending lawsuits.

Companies know that it requires full documentation based on facts to successfully defend the firm. As an employee, you want to be especially careful about any type of performance that lends itself to indisputable and factual numbers such as the following:

1. Number of days absent
2. Number of days tardy
3. Number of late reports
4. Number of customer complaints

5. Percent of sales objectives achieved
6. Percent of production goals achieved
7. Percent of defects
8. Percent of expenditures over budget
9. Degree of profitability

Job security requires that your performance remains within the acceptable numbers at all times.

PAYING FOR PERFORMANCE

The current practice is to disassociate performance appraisals from salary administration. Apparently, it is believed that managers will be more objective in rating employees when there is not an implication of a direct salary relationship.

A very definite correlation should exist between ratings of employee performance and compensation. If an employer is not using performance appraisals as a direct method of determining compensation, the question arises as to what method is being used. If salary administration is not based on performance, is it based on the type of clothing worn, the make of car driven, or the home location?

In times of limited pay increases, raises are often distributed by broad percentages rather than specific performance. Both achievers and nonachievers are placed into one big bell-shaped compensation curve. For example, if top management decides on a 4 percent overall salary increase, then pay raises for virtually everyone will fall in the 3 to 5 percent range. By trying to keep all employees relatively happy, the nonachievers benefit at the expense of the achievers.

The increasing competitiveness of American business and the urgent need for improved productivity will encourage smart companies to go back to basics and distribute salary increases to deserving individuals on the basis of performance.

Smart employees will keep an accurate record of their pay increases. It can always be argued that pay increases are never given to persons who are performing at a totally unacceptable level.

DOCUMENTING NEGATIVE PERFORMANCE

If you are an evaluator, never place in writing such phrases as "should . . ." or "needs to . . ." or "fails to . . ." without including documentation. Phrases of this type should always be followed with a clarifying statement, such as "as evidenced by your reports being late five times during the past six months" or "because you were absent fourteen days during the past six months." Simply making an indirect criticism without corresponding documentation can be devastating to a company in a court of law.

An evaluation practice that many managers improperly follow is to bring up undesirable incidents at appraisal time. When an improper incident occurs, managers have a tendency to place a note in the appraisal file.

Sometimes incidents are brought up an entire year after they have occurred. The employee may have understandably forgotten the details and quickly becomes defensive. Effective managers discuss problems immediately with employees and never wait to spring them during appraisal time.

Smart employees will periodically ask their bosses how well they are doing. This tactic places the superior in a position where it is difficult to later criticize an employee who has previously taken the initiative to inquire about their performance.

Another undesirable practice is to turn personal evaluation sessions into a review of the company's condition. Many managers find it easier to talk about the company's performance, than the employee's performance. The purpose of the evaluation session is to review employee performance, and the company's condition should be discussed in separate meetings.

During the appraisal interview, smart employees will try to sit next to their superior. You want to convey the impression that you are a vital team member trying to improve your performance for your mutual benefit. Sitting across from the superior creates an undesirable psychological barrier.

The best managers view evaluations as an ongoing process and continuously let subordinates know how they are doing. They give praise at every opportunity and immediately advise subordinates of areas where improvement is needed. Subordinates working for a real manager never face evaluation time with apprehension because they already know where they stand.

You should take performance appraisals very seriously. It's important that you do your very best to earn the highest possible rating. If you are a manager, it's also essential that you evaluate subordinates in the fairest and most objective manner. Always rate every one of your subordinates at the same time because your ratings can be influenced by your health, your present problems, or even the weather.

Managers should be coaches, not judges!

USING ENTREPRENEURSHIP AS A SAFETY NET

The ever-present possibility of a takeover, merger, or downsizing program is making organizational life increasingly unsettled for more and more employees.

You have control over many things in your life. You can select the house of your choice, the best mortgage program, the best investment plan for your children's education, etc. You can have everything on target to the best of your ability. At a time when all is well, you can jump into your car one morning and hear on the radio that XYZ Company has just issued a tender offer to purchase your employer.

In the advent of a takeover, all bets are off. You may feel that only the high rollers lose their jobs in times of a takeover. Don't count on it.

You may feel, for example, that your employer will always have an order department because it has existed since the company was founded. However, an acquiring company with its massive computers may view your product line as one that can easily be merged into their direct order entry processing at a computer located on the other side of the country.

Customer service may be transferred outside of the country. Persons using the 800 number may actually be talking to someone in Australia, India, or the Caribbean.

Takeovers affect everyone equally. You, your superior, and your superior's boss are quickly reduced to equal terms. All the hard work and relationships that you have built over the years suddenly become worthless. An acquiring company will do whatever it wants with no explanations necessary.

PROSPERING WITH SIDELINE ENTREPRENEURSHIP

In view of the growing uncertainty of organizational life, it is not surprising that more and more full-time hourly and salaried workers are becoming sideline entrepreneurs. The author has known many employees who have run a variety of sideline ventures ranging from fishing lures to wall plates to publishing. Parallel careers among employees are no doubt reaching record levels in America.

For most people, it is becoming increasingly unlikely that they can accumulate a substantial net worth as an employee. Entrepreneurship has never been easier, with the Internet providing worldwide markets from your home office.

Persons who engage in sideline businesses often work at a hectic pace during evenings, weekends, and vacations. The sideline entrepreneur looks to areas outside the job for greater satisfaction, challenges, opportunities, financial rewards, and true security.

Moreover, individuals with sideline businesses benefit from numerous tax advantages that are not available to typical employees.

As employees become more educated, they are better prepared to engage in outside ventures. Personal computers with their well-designed business software are facilitating the entrepreneurship movement.

Entrepreneurship provides a striking contrast to the highly regimented and bureaucratic environment of large organizations. The ability to make every decision is a gratifying experience after a day at the office where virtually all activities are governed by policies and procedures.

In a sideline business, all your energies can be devoted to making the enterprise successful with no concern for office politics or game playing. Entrepreneurship provides the opportunity to be totally responsible for the success of your efforts.

Sideline entrepreneurs realize that career planning in large organizations is becoming more uncertain. They recognize that security comes from independence, and persons who operate a profitable sideline venture are not placing their entire livelihood at the whim of corporate managers.

Spouses and other family members often become actively involved in sideline businesses. A joint team effort to build a prosperous business can be a very exciting and rewarding experience. It can provide the highest degree of unlimited growth potential and security.

Operating a sideline business should not interfere in any way with your primary job. A person who comes to work after spending half the night manufacturing a product or shipping orders is not being fair to the employer.

Because of legal reasons, moonlighters need to be sure that they are not competing with their employer for clients, information, or customers.

Smart corporate employees channel their efforts for the benefit of the organization. In a sideline business, you work for the benefit of yourself.

ADDING IT UP

The ability to capably perform your job is simply not sufficient for attaining job security. You need to combine technical competence with political shrewdness and a degree of personal effectiveness that achieves results and attracts the attention of your superiors.

You need to tactfully toot your own horn. Become a public relations agent for yourself and your department. One way to gain recognition for you and your department is to gain publicity in all house organs and publications.

Send reports of your successes to company editors who are always looking for good stories and pictures. Annual reports are increasingly emphasizing human resources.

People will treat you in the same manner as you treat them. If you are positive, confident and enthusiastic you will be treated as such.

Keep in mind the story of a bag handler at a major airport. The handler accidentally dropped a person's luggage. The owner was furious and criticized the handler in no uncertain terms. Later, a bystander told the handler that it was terrible the way he was treated. The handler looked up and said, "Oh, don't worry about me. That gentleman is going to London but his luggage is going to Singapore!"

Never relate improved benefits to job security. Longer vacation periods, for example, are usually granted on the basis of seniority, not performance.

Keep objective about your job security and avoid acquiring one year's experience many times. Don't let yourself get caught in a comfortable rut.

Take charge of your future because you cannot rely on others. Never tie your job security to a single person or nebulous function. The best job security is your employability and capability of becoming a successful entrepreneur.

You have to make things happen. If you want greater responsibility, let it be known. If you want a certain job, go for it.

Select several of your strengths and maximize them to the fullest. If you write well, then write. If you speak well, then speak.

Develop a tremendous amount of confidence in selected traits. As you gain competence, you develop greater self-esteem. If you think well of yourself, you will project a positive image of competence.

Develop your mental skills and application so that others will consider you to be sharp and smart. Display superior powers of comprehension and be capable of sustaining a high level of concentration. Use common sense and learn to think fast on your feet.

Strive to make greater use of your mental powers by widening your intellectual interests. Remember that the human brain is largely unused and is capable of producing at a much higher rate than normal output.

Display an inquisitive mind and keep alert to the world around you. Be capable of discussing current events, balance of trade, or the latest game scores.

Maintain control over your ego and concentrate on achieving results. Do not believe that the world revolves around you. Focus on the big picture and do not confuse activity with accomplishment. Keep life in perspective and display a good sense of humor.

Follow a diversified life style and keep physically active and mentally fit. Develop a reputation for being a deep thinker with a sharp mind that is quick, alert, and responsive.

Above all, be positive. Make a habit of spreading good news throughout the organization. Train your mind to think success, not failure. Never make excuses because of age, health, education, etc.

If you are wrong, admit it and move on. If you incur a setback, use it as a springboard and bounce back with tremendous energy.

Think and act like a secure leader. Use positive and uplifting words at every opportunity. Be a dynamo of enthusiasm. Think out of the box and think big!

Display attitudes that are extremely positive but also realistic. Develop self-confidence, take risks, and don't be afraid to occasionally fail. Keep learning and adhere to a philosophy of life that reflects high personal values and goals.

If you are a manager, delegate to increase your effectiveness and develop people. Strive to be results oriented and give positive reinforcement and recognition to others. Think big and expect the best.

In every group of equally talented people, the individuals who maintain a political awareness will often win out. You need to recognize and effectively work with the political dynamics that are present in all organizations.

You need to excel in professional excellence. You have a unique background that is possessed by no one else. By recognizing the changes that are occurring in organizational life, you can build on your strengths and develop the qualities needed to achieve your highest goals and job security.

About the Author

James E. Neal, Jr., holds a B.B.A. degree from the University of Toledo and a M.A. degree from the Institute of Labor and Industrial Relations of the University of Illinois. He has served in management human resources positions with a major international corporation. He founded Neal Publications, Inc., in 1978 and is the author of seven books including the best-selling *Effective Phrases for Performance Appraisals*, which has appeared on a number of national best-seller lists.

INDEX

activity *versus*
    accomplishment, 96
administrative assistants,
    70, 72
administrative
    effectiveness, 97–100
alcohol consumption, 47
approval authority, 74–75
arriving early at the
    office, 55, 95
assertiveness, 34–35
assistants, as sign of
    overstaffing, 13–14
authority, 54, 74–75
authority, lines of, 57

bad news, announcing, 88
bargaining power, 20
bookies (employee
    type), 28
brainstorming, 65
budgeting, 59–60
business travel,
    94–95

career choices, 16–18
certified automotive
    technicians, 17
cliques, 82–83
"closed door syn-
    drome," 86
college graduates, under-
    employment of, 15–16
communication network,
    employee, 87
communications, as
    college major, 16
communication skills,
    85–91
company publications,
    87, 117
competency, 63–64, 120
complainers (employee
    type), 27–28
"computer depend-
    ency," 98
confidentiality, 46
continuing education,
    78–79

convention, show or conference goers (employee type), 31–32

corporate developments, communicating, 88

corporate trouble warning signs, 10–13

corporation, new, 1–5

cost containment, 58, 60

creativity, 64–65

credit for accomplishments, 36

criticism, 45–46, 49, 65

customer complaints, 80–81

customer service, 4, 42, 100

danger signals
  corporate, 10–13
  personal, 25–26

decision-making, 42, 60–62, 94

dedication, 104–106

delegation, 69–75, 120

dependability, 38

diplomacy, 65–66

disappointments, 44–45

discrimination lawsuits, 108, 110

do-it-yourselfers (employee type), 29

downsizing, 7–10

dress standards, 38–39

drifters (employee type), 28

dual reporting relationships, 58

education, continuing, 78–79

educational choices, 15–18

effectiveness, administrative, 97–100

egomaniacs (employee type), 26–27

e-mails, "for your information," 85

Emerson, Ralph Waldo, 37

employee communication network, 87

employee evaluation system, 20–21, 107–111

employees
  front-line, 81
  overseas, 4–5, 17, 114
  rapport with, 67
  recognizing, 36, 66
  senior, 20–23
  temporary, 3
  terminating, 7–10
  types, 26–32
  vital, 33–51

employer, monitoring, 10–13

employment discrimination lawsuits, 108, 110

enthusiasm, 36, 37, 119

entrepreneurship, 113–116

ethics, 116

farming, 18

form letters, 66

"for your information" e-mails, 85

front-line employees, 81

gossip, 89
graphic arts, 17

handwritten notes, 66
healthcare, as career
    field, 16–17
high school math and
    science teachers, 17
holidays, 96
hot shots (employee
    type), 29
house organs, 87, 117
humor, 49, 90

image building, 26–32
initiative, 37
international trade,
    4–5, 78
Internet, 3, 17, 114
interviewing, 86
intra-company billing, 11
intuitive judgment, 63

job descriptions, 43–44
job security
    factors affecting, 1–5,
        16–18
    levels, 19–23
job titles, 72
joiners (employee
    type), 31
jokers (employee
    type), 28
judgment, 62–63

knowledge, 77–83

lawsuits, employment
    discrimination,
    108, 110
leadership traits, 55
letters, form, 66

"librarians" (employee
    type), 30–31
listening, 86
loyalty, 104–106

mail room clerks, 87
management skills,
    53–67
managers, new, 53–55
manufacturing, 17–18
math teachers, 17
maturity, 44–45
medical technolo-
    gists, 17
meetings, 93–94
merit pay, 109–110
monitoring your
    employer, 10–13
morticians, 17
motivation, 35–37

names, recalling, 66
negative people, 49
negative performance,
    documenting,
    110–111
networking, 78, 80, 82
new managers, strategies
    for, 53–55
notes, handwritten, 66
numerical documentation,
    in performance
    appraisals, 108–109
nurses, 17

objectives, setting,
    102–104
oral expression, 89–91
organizing, 56–57
outsourcing, 2, 3
over-delegators (employee
    type), 29

overseas employees, 4–5,
17, 114
overstaffing, 13–14

paperwork, 98–99
paying for performance,
109–110
performance appraisals,
20–21, 107–111
personal danger signals,
25–26
personality traits, 33–34
personal problems,
46–47
pharmacists, 17, 18
physical appearance,
38–39
physical therapists, 17
physician assistants, 18
planning, 56
position descriptions,
43–44
positive communications,
89, 91
positive people, 36, 37,
49–50, 119
positive thinkers, 33–34,
81, 119
production person-
nel, 108
professional associa-
tions, 78
professionalism, 38–39,
63–64
promotions, 20, 53–55
publications, profes-
sional, 78

quality of work, 42–43
quantity of work, 43

rapport with em-
ployees, 67

realistic thinkers, 81, 119
recognition of employees,
36, 66
reporting, as symptom of
overstaffing, 11–12
reporting relation-
ships, 58
reports, financial, 10–11,
80, 88–89
resumes, 41
retirement incentives,
22–23
robots, 17
rumors, 86–87

salary administration,
109–110
sales personnel, 81, 108
scheduling time, 94–96
science teachers, 17
secretaries, 54, 63, 70,
72, 87
selling, 3, 43
senior employees, 20–23
socializing, 50–51
speaking ability, 89–91
"status quo" people
(employee type), 30
staying late at the
office, 95
stress management,
48–50
superiors
keeping informed, 85
vacations of, 71

tact, 65–66
team players, 34–35
technology
and entrepreneur-
ship, 114
impact on job
security, 2

keeping up with,
97–100
and stress, 48
telephone operators, 87
temporary employees, 3
terminating employees,
7–10
time management, 93–96
titles, job, 72
trade, international,
4–5, 78
trade associations, 78
travel, business, 94–95
travelers (employee
type), 31
troubled companies,
recognizing, 10–14

vacations of superiors, as
opportunity, 71

versatility, 40–41
vocational schools, 16

warning signs
corporate, 10–13
personal, 25–26
work area appearance, 39
working with others,
34–35
workplace changes, 1–5
work quality, 42–43
work quantity, 43
writing ability, 91

"yes" people (employee
type), 30

NOTES

NOTES

NOTES